PHENOMENAL CHANGE

Empowering Your Subconscious Mind to Create Your Change

Gloria B. Daniels

Copyright © 2021 by Gloria Daniels
Los Angeles, California
All rights reserved.
Printed and Bound in the United States of America

Published and Distributed By
HER Horizon Publishing House
Los Angeles, California
Email: danielsgloria37@gmail.com

Packaging/Consulting
Professional Publishing House
1425 W. Manchester Ave. Ste B Los Angeles, California 90047 323-750-3592
Email: professionalpublishinghouse@yahoo.com
www.Professionalpublishinghouse.com

First printing August 2021
978-0-578-96298-6
10987654321

No part of this book may be reproduced, stored in a retrieval system or transmitted in any form or by any means without the prior written permission of the publisher—except by a reviewer who may quote brief passages in a review to be printed in a newspaper, magazine or journal. For inquiry contact the publisher: danielsgloria37@gmail.com

Acknowledgments

My thanks to the world…

Thanks for having a change of heart to keep this world turning on its axis positively. To the people who helped make my life a living reality with their positive influence, you know who you are, and how you treated me along the way through this assimilation, thanks for being an example by showing your unconditional love, it helped me expand in such a way.

To Devon E. Edmond, Sr., a divine thank you goes out to you, my beloved brother, who told me to research everything I believe in and make sure it holds facts and truth to my journey's walk of life that I am experiencing. Yes, he was on point to challenge my phenomenal change of heart and thoughts that were desperately needed to know myself. Yeses that was my beginning to soul search, and question everything and everyone, I let in my life, yes I did just that, and found my true self waiting for me to believe in myself, yes I'm forever grateful my beloved soulmate, rest in power.

Thanks to my mother, Lucille Daniels, who was my hardest critic, who pushed me to prove myself to her, and most of all, to prove to myself eye have the will to do so… or wait for a handout, she always told me don't just talk about it be about it.

To a dear friend, Cliff B. Louis, who said to me, "I don't know where I would be if you had not come along in my life to help me make it through this midlife crisis." Yes, I'm one of his witnesses to his phenomenal change in his mental and physical mindset that was desperately needed for the better for his life journey and others. Sharing a part of his journey for a moment showed me many individuals desperately need love and support on getting headed in the right direction.

A special thanks to Barbara Lindsey, who said to me and a room full of people, "I would never judge people who are dealing with life-changing dilemmas like sickness and health issues." She said she would never judge any person on how they deal with getting rid of any pain. You don't know what it is like until you go through it. Her statement is 100% facts.

This divine thanks goes out to sister Ruby Robinson, who said to me, "Sister Gloria, never be ashamed to praise the God in you. Do so by loving the world and receiving what God has for you." She said, "No one can receive what was intended for you by the grace of God." I always carry those words of wisdom in my heart she spoke to me.

A very grateful thanks to brother Cordelle Candler, who told me to keep my eyes focused on things above, and not the things in the world, it's below you, but keep your eyes on the prize it's in the upper room of thought, that was one of the best-seeded statement he planted into my life, 20 years ago...he said don't eat the poison in the world grow it the natural way...

To my children Trusion, Maloura, Rogrick, Kaysha, Elijah, Eniya, Isaac, Isaiah, a phenomenal thank you for being the center of my reasoning for the world to change their hearts, from a negative perspective to a positive one. I think about this world you will inherit from every conscience decision that is made and created by us all, and I choose to help ... Thanks for being a part of this matrix with me, none of you asked to be here born into this assimilation all eight of you, but my reality is eye gave birth into this place and space eight times leaving my blueprint through all of you, it's in your bloodline and DNA, generation after generation I will be there, thanks for being a part of me, Indeed, I am you all in this phenomenal change, in this world.

Forevermore.... YOUR MOTHER....

The thanks I gave to these individuals are because they were my drive to keep going. They were all I could think about and why it was so important to leave this message to their present life, they shared with me. They alone made my world change inside and out on the kind of influence I wanted to leave on the world, so I give back the same seeds they planted in me. Now Is it ok that I pass down the sacred seeds of love, nothing to plant in a garden with the physical hands but plant them in your heart and thoughts with your conscience where you will feel and see infinite growth within yourself that will bring about great beauty here in the Garden of Eden. I was always told beauty is in the eye of the beholder, and indeed I behold their beauty in my heart, to change the world inside of me first, and in there I find the true love for the world.... I HAD A PHENOMENAL CHANGE.... I HEARD THE KNOCK AND I ANSWERED THE DOOR... WILL YOU?

Table of Contents

Introduction 9

Chapter 1: The Meaning of Phenomenal
Change and Knowing the Mind is All 13

Chapter 2: The Seven Principles for the
World to Change 17

Chapter 3: The Divine All, We are One 31

Chapter 4: Sorrow Change 36

Chapter 5: Social Change 57

Chapter 6: Times Change 94

Chapter 7: World Change 113

Chapter 8: Believe in You! You Matter! 132

Chapter 9: Healthier for Your Change 140

Chapter 10: God's Love 149

My Mission Statement 152

INTRODUCTION

To my readers, I am so excited for you to take this journey of a lifetime, to empower your subconscious mind, to enlighten you on the powers of thought. We are amazing mentally, physically, and spiritually. Yes, we are phenomenal beings that have been born into this dimension of mental consciousness that vibrates off everything we say and do. We are consistently and rapidly moving throughout this life, expanding every day.

Channeling from one side of consciousness to the other side of thought, then action to sum it all up. This life journey of ours is full of excitement and mysteries I am proud to unveil and enlighten you on the knowledge that empowers my everyday walk of *life* and my phenomenal change.

Yes, this is something I had to write about in this lifetime. As we experience this journey, your truth and experience will prove facts, how you lived your life. I am sharing with you, not for self-gratification but ordered by the instructions of the Divine All and the universal message.

It is my calling to share the phenomenal change you are designed to partake in. This is the universal energy of life that we all experience every day. Everything in existence, seen and unseen, is connected, inseparable from one another to a field of our Divine Oneness. All of humanity is universal oneness. We are connected by a super natural force, designed by the Divine All.

The mental mind is everywhere at once. The mind is *all* and creates all images around you. It moves through all things, living or material. The mind is the only true reality in its entire existence. This wormhole is the infinite conductor that portals in our thoughts, of which we use those thoughts daily to manifest our reality. All things and decisions are made right there in the mind. Yes, the mind is infinite. The mind moves and so does the universal knowledge and good forces of mental power move in the mind.

Phenomenal change is mental and infinite and always available to us all. Let us be very aware of the universal law and be honored to increase our awareness of it. The divine energy and its divine present want to give you this gift; to know the truth about our illuminating powers and our human ability. Like our super cognition, the powers to self-heal, and much more.

Yes, these abilities also can give you the power to defeat an evil mindset by simply connecting the powers between the mind and the heart, creating a unity that would allow you to break free from a defeated mindset. Cognition is present when you allow the heart and the mind to be one. These powers are real. It's one of my favorable manifestations. I indulge in it on a daily, defeating any negative mindset. Yes, this force of positivity, this angelic energy, is invested in you and me now, forever.

The Divine All created the mind with thoughts and actions, showing how phenomenal we are. This message is about your phenomenal change. We have the power to change the way we think on an epic scale, based on mental conscience that is based on psychology mentalism. I realize and understand as humans we are phenomenal beings with much to offer, and have offered on an epic scale in this lifetime. I believe in every person on this planet to change their thinking from a negative perception to a positive mindset to broaden the horizons of thoughts, feelings, and actions for the good of all humanity. Everyone born into humanity has a moral responsibility to know themselves on an epic scale. Humanity must know that all of us govern and shape the world we live in today. Our thoughts are one of a kind, and that's a fact. What we think plays an epic role in our lives, and I believe we can have a phenomenal change, mentally, physically, spiritually, and even emotionally. If we pay attention to this assimilation we live in and pay attention to the universal law of love, this world will be a better place to inhabit generation after generation. Infinity and beyond will bring new meaning, an inspiration to this dimension to explore. I believe, and envision this to be so, with the help of your mentalism, and one love for all human life, yes, we all count.

CHAPTER 1

The Meaning of Phenomenal Change and Knowing the Mind is All

The words "phenomenal" and "change" hold their own power, and that's a fact. These two words together hold remarkable actions that will last a lifetime. Let me break "phenomenal" and "change" down and then build your awareness up to empower your journey.

I'm about to unveil to you the words "phenomenal" and "change" and yes, I am talking about your phenomenal change. When you hear the word "phenomenal," you think of greatness off top. It sounds like the best of everything. You can clearly hear the magic it holds. Wow, sounds exciting, doesn't it? This word is very inspiring and something you will want to experience every day.

When I hear "phenomenal," I get a warm sensation all over my body that tells me everything about the word is divine. Let's get a closer look at this word to know exactly what we are dealing with on an epic scale.

The word "phenomenal" is an adjective. It means "very remarkable; extraordinary," and if you go into the synonyms, it unveils similar words like exceptional, remarkable, outstanding, amazing, astonishing, stunning, staggering, marvelous, magnificent, wonderful, breathtaking, believable, uncommon, rare, mind-boggling, mind blowing, and the list goes on and on.

I'm going to stop there before I lose your attention on the importance of the word, and need I say I am talking about **you**, yes you right now, holding this message in your hand. This is about you and the Divine All. I'm revealing this message to you to keep that phenomenal energy going that is invested in your bloodline.

DNA doesn't lie, and neither does phenomenal change. It's something you can always count on.

Now we are going to jump into the word "change." It is just as powerful as "phenomenal." It's how you perceive the word in action. "Change" is one of the most divine words on the face of this planet ordered by the Divine All.

The word "change" can be viewed as a very positive word, but many perceive it as a negative. It's how you perceive it in your mind on your day to day walk of life.

The word "change" for me is very powerful. It is an action that consistently moves without being ordered to "stop." Can you let what I said just sink in for a moment? Let us analyze this word more thoughtfully so we can get the full view of how powerful this word is in your life.

The definition of the word "change" is used to describe an action, state of occurrence, forming the main part, of a story, or sentence, such as "becoming" or "happening." The definition is "Make or become different." The synonym is "transmuting." Change is also a transformation also ordered in nature. To get you to see your change from a phenomenal point of view, showing you how to open your mind to alchemy, better known as the transformation of matter, to find the "Universal Elixir" also known as the truth and your experience. The KYBALION teaches us that the mind is all.

"The principle of mentalism" and on this plane of consciousness we are dealing with seven principles that embody the truth about the phenomenal change. Nothing stays the same. We must know that mentalism is one of the most important attributes to our phenomenal walk of life. The mind holds all keys to your everyday experience on what you think and how you should go by doing things each passing day. Children are not exempt; they also can possess a very positive and powerful mind. The mind is a tool in this universe. You can do nothing without it, my readers. Your mentalism is one of the greatest gifts from the Divine All that you can possess in this assimilation, dimension, life, journey…whatever you want to call it. The message is here, all your decisions are based there, housed right in the upper room of thought. Never forget: "The mind is All." Let me explain by sharing how the universe is mental and it works according to your phenomenal change, not just mine but every person on the planet plays a major role in the mental affect. As I stated before, the universe works through our thoughts and actions, and that's a fact. Daily, we are consistently shifting and shaping our world outwardly, and manifesting, phenomenal change, with thoughts, from the White House, all the way to the poverty parts of the world, the illusion is abroad and yes, we all play, a part of our world appearance, under the terms of mentalism and mental change.

CHAPTER 2

The Seven Principles for the World to Change

1. The Principle of Mentalism
2. The Principle of Correspondence
3. The Principle of Vibration
4. The Principle of Polarity
5. The Principle of Rhythm
6. The Principle of Cause and Effect
7. The Principle of Gender

If everyone acknowledges their mental role in this world and follow these principles, they will see the many changes that are designed to shape our reality. Every day there is something new happening, with someone, at some time or another. Someone will hear about something happening, and someone will always have a story to tell, no matter if it's true or not. For instance, stories like Nipsey Hussle, Kobe Bryant, COVID-19, and George Floyd. Stories like this will be told and right then we will see our connection to the Universal Oneness, as we all feel the effects that were forced on society, as we journey throughout this assimilation we call life.

The phenomenal change is taking place as you read, without any of your physical efforts. Yes, reading is all mental effort, and so is the change; it's all mental effort as well.

<u>*The Principle of Correspondence*</u>—is always in effect with phenomenal change. There is always something going on around us. It could be life being born or it could be life being taken away, by death or hoax, but yes, it is always some kind of change. Getting a job or losing a job, buying a home, or losing a home, change is happening; it never stops.

Many people often say, "As Above so Below, so Below as Above." The true meaning of "As Above" refers to the universe outside; space; the cosmos; your thoughts. "As below" refers to the physical world, the physical body, the physical things you do and say is all the soul below. Another great phrase is, "What a man thinks, so he or she is."

Your thoughts create your reality, which is why it's so important, in this lifetime, to know thyself.

The mind is All, and it is always going through some type of change. "Thoughts held in mind produce after their own kind" is a very old and wise phrase to follow. The phrase teaches you to watch what you think and to keep your mind focused on positive things that you want to see happen in your reality, not the opposite of what you don't want to see.

Why put negative thoughts in your mind to create fear and chaos on the outside of your body with negative actions? Do you want to take fear, hatred, pain into your future? So, remember, "Thoughts held in mind produce after their own kind," good or bad, your thoughts make a difference in your perception of your life.

Thoughts held in mind are the law of the mind in action. It never sits still, always moving and changing, each moment, second by second, with all kinds of influence, good and bad; it changes you inside and out. There is always a thought to build up something, and a thought to tear down. There's an inflow, there's an outflow. There's action and there's a reaction. How many know this to be a fact?

Nothing endures, but changes, and thoughts, we must understand the truth; nothing stays the same. We all will face correspondence in this lifetime. Many of us have already faced it, and were not aware of the phenomenal change, involving correspondence.

The Principle of Vibration holds all evidence that we are not always aware that nothing rests. Everything moves, or always happens, and everything vibrates, around us because of our thoughts; they become action. So, we are always in motion, and manifestation is always taking place with us. The pendulum swings back and forth, therefore we are always in motion. The energy you put in anything; your mind will manifest. "THE MIND IS ALL." it never sleeps. Our mind is consistently moving during the night. The evidence is our dreams and that's a fact. As the body lay still, the mind is moving in and out of time on other planes. Facts show everything is dual or has duality, good versus evil in the mind.

<u>The Principle of Polarity</u> teaches us that everything has its place, and there is always a force of nature happening, and change is all around us nonstop. The amazement about this principal "Polarity," also teaches us that everything has its opposites, that's why it looks as if nothing is happening around us, but it is my readers, it is. We as individuals say, "I'm not going through nothing," because we know everything is, and isn't, at the same time, if that makes sense at all.

We all know there is always two sides to a story, negative and positive. There are two poles, therefore, we are always changing. I'm talking about phenomenal change, family, and friends.

Everything we do in this world is by design. It may seem hard to believe, but it is facts. "Polarity" shows us that manifestation in this lifetime is a two-way street.

Let me put it more straightforward, we deal with light and darkness, which are the same different poles, when you are experiencing, phenomenal change, like, where does darkness leave off, and where does light begin? what is the difference, between hard and soft, between black and white, between high and low? That's the question, can you see the difference in the degrees?

This principle of polarity operates on the mental plane to show you there are two degrees in the opposites of words, and one of them has a better outcome, When the word is used at that moment, polarity teaches us when it comes to words, there is always a value, and an importance's, at the time any word is used. For instance, "I hate to hear someone was killed" by someone or something, I use the word "Hate." It has a value and degree; it's all how you use the word and your mentalism to bring about your change of thought and then action to sum it all up.

The mentalism needs to over stand the changes that are taking place in the mind with this divine message from the "ALL." I know at this point you can feel the change taking place; your energy has changed because you are phenomenal, and you have been called to make a difference in all of humanity; what an honor to know that mentalism plays a role in our atmosphere.

Polarity teaches us in history that something is written it is read by someone and the message went forward, but not always acted on due to each individual or the state of their mentalism at that moment in life. Polarity teaches that the way you use your thoughts can cause a real consequence of an action, or something happening negatively, if you are not careful with your thoughts, that's why it's important, to know the mind is a powerful tool in this universe. If you didn't know this before now, well it's been revealed.

This message you are receiving is to keep you from falling for all kinds of traps, and illusions, and mental attacks throughout your life. Phenomenal change shows us everything flows out and in, and many things rise and fall in your life. But the pendulum of life swings back and forth, and the rhythm never loses a beat in our phenomenal journey.

The Principle of Rhythm embodies the truth, that everything manifests, as a measured motion, that's what I am pointing out, we are always keeping up with the rhythm of life. It may not seem like it, but we are.

As our hearts beat with the rhythm that says we are a part of this world, we can feel that we are in line with the universe.

The beat of our heart gives every person reference, they are alive and a living soul. Rhythm changes according to our thoughts. I'm going to share an example of how rhythm is always present. This 2020-2021 COVID-19 pandemic has caused a great rhythm, all over the world. It has changed the world forever, due to the fear that was placed in the minds of people and atmosphere, all around the world.

This pandemic is a prime example of what I am sharing with you all, how powerful the mind is.

It could be used for good or evil, but most definitely the rhythm, of this COVID-19 wicked plan, to depopulate, humanity by any means necessary, it seems as though the plan has worked and still is being dragged out, with the full perception, that everyone should be afraid, for their life.

This perception that your God has no power over the coronavirus, and we are all counted as sheep, for the slaughter is right here in your face, from what it looks like. All they need you to do is obey the television, also known as "Tell lies to your vision," a man-made perception of what they want your reality to consist of from someone else's thoughts and point of view to implement clinical trial vaccines that don't cure the virus, so at this point, you are being told to trust what someone else says, they think is best for you even if it's not good for you.

COVID-19 has taken the rhythm of the planet into a whole new tune that is on a very low vibration, that threatens all of humanity, mentally, physically, spiritually, and emotionally.

Therefore, the rhythm changes, according to our thoughts, until we all embody the death transition, changing from one state to another. More importantly, we know everything living on this planet has a rhythm and plays a role today.

Everything matters on this planet, all of us play epic roll sunup to sundown. It is an honor to rise and shine with a healthy mindset, to walk in peace, balance, harmony, order, reciprocity, propriety, justice, and the list could go on and on, but you get the point. The mentalism needs to inner stand, the change that needs to take place to receive the Divine's message and act on it. Yes, all words are spells within themselves, sending a clear message to whoever needs the message, any time in life.

At this moment in life right now this message is for you, whoever is ready to experience life like never before, by trusting yourself 100% and knowing that this phenomenal change is right for you right now. This message holds a balance of life, and rhythm, that has its cause and its affected, and we know every cause has its effect, and every effect has its cause.

Everything happens according to the law; nothing escapes the universal law that's facts. When I speak on nothing escapes universal law, what I am talking about are the cause and effect. What you put in is what you get out in this world. Nothing happens, just to happen. Everything going on in this world, positive or comes from the principle of cause and effect.

Cause and Effect is a very powerful principle. The changes we face often are because what we do and say causes an effect in this universe. No matter if it's on television or in music, books, news, they all make the cause and the effect on this planet.

To get a better grip on this principle, and the message, think about the cause and effect that you have been creating over the years of your life. I encourage everyone to put a better cause and positive effect in the world it is much needed on an epic scale. It's best to raise the planet and create the best, effect you can create in life.

When it comes to phenomenal, it's in everyone's interest to be a mover, and not a pawn being used, for someone else wicked plans and pleasure, I would never encourage anyone to be a pawn, when you elevate your mind positively, a new world emerges in your present life that's a universal law, if you choose to be a pawn you lose anyway that's also universal law. So why not affect your life and everyone that you encounter with positive energy? It will bring more peace to humanity, something we all need.

We all can agree to that. Being positive can gain you great wealth, it can benefit you now, and it can benefit you in the afterlife, and that's facts, so embrace phenomenal change positively. In today's world, it doesn't matter, if you are male or female gender, it manifests on all planes in this simulation.

The Principle of Gender—Masculine and feminine are always at work, physically, mentally, and spiritually when it comes to the physical plane. It's all about the sex origin,

God origin, of how one gender can be without the other is the question but what is more important.

Is God a word? Yes, it is. Apparently about 2,500 years old to be exact from what the QUORA dictionary says. It was first used around 600 AD. This word was said to have come from the Germans. It came out of the word "Gott," which means "to invoke." The word "invoke" means "call upon," an entity, (spiritually) usually a God, Goddess, etc. to protect you, heal you and give you strength or even power. The University of Theologians say they have studied all the sources of religion and the origin of God.

It's very epic to compare the different religions in a knowledgeable way, without having to go in a debate with someone, and do it in a balanced way.

God the word, is the head of all religion and has been made a male gender. But God the deity, of human existence, the creator of life from the beginning that source, that created the first human existence, that God it's not limitless, it has, no gender but mankind has limited The Creator on an epic scale with putting gender on God as he.

God, the word, is something limited. It's something you should think long and hard about when you put gender on God.

With this phenomenal creation of man and woman on this planet, it has those principles, of those two phenomenal genders. But God, The Creator, Higher

Power, Supreme One, The All…however you describe that image of your God in your mind, it should never be placed in a bound expression of life, like the two genders that exist here, that woman creates. So, the spelling of the word God hasn't been around long. Yes, there was a creator long before the word (God) came into existence, 2,500 years ago so you can't put a gender on God because it will become a personal conflict.

To find out for yourself, it's right at your local library or your fingertips by studying online. It's also a very beneficial way to learn historical theology. I encourage you to study, to know where your origin and roots come from.

Moving back into the vortex of gender, so is the male or female a creation made from God? And does God have a gender? This is very epic; the conscious energy of this point of view is very powerful, well the male and female origin manifest everywhere, yes, we are a part of nature in every way imaginable. Creation can only come in these forms, supernatural of a manifestation attributed by force male and female.

Beyond scientific understanding, the supernatural exists in everything. It's impossible to create life without thoughts or information that is passed through the DNA, then action to create the life. As they say, thoughts held in mind produce after their own kind. How many know this to be fact and truth? Everything and everyone has two elements: masculine and feminine matters, and these two genders share those qualities when it is something being created.

We often name it with a male or female criterion like a child created by a woman in her womb supernatural. The two sexes—male and female gender—are supernatural but only one gender can be born again through their own body and be born in the form of male or female gender, and only the woman can do that. How phenomenal is that?

Women have the biggest role in this world, which is the greatest gift of all roles on this planet—to be the mother of all living souls. As they are born into this world, the true-life giver is the woman, and yes, it's natural the way it was originally designed. Everything that grows in nature is designed without your permission—trees, flowers, and grass never ask for permission to grow, it just does. There is a supernatural phenomenon that takes place in and out of season, and females and males express themselves all over the world from sea to shining sea. You will see the males and females in nature doing what they have always done, without permission and that is to continue to grow expand and create beauty unimaginable, we all know the phrase" beauty is in the eye of the beholder" that's facts."

The "Divine All" planned it like this in this lifetime to give the supernatural role to the woman, not a machine to create life, only a woman can make a human being any gender inside of her body for 40 weeks. The woman creates the male gender on this plane no doubt. The XY chromosome always starts off as female for the first two months and by the third month of pregnancy, the sex of the fetus can change from female to male or stay female gender in the womb. The woman is the main conductor of all genders of human life on this planet, she is designed very phenomenally by the "Divine All." The woman is the phenomenal creator of all human life. The change takes place in her mind and then her body. How extraordinary is the woman to make the male gender exist? Yes, nature made it that way for a reason, yet the man, the male gender is the main conductor taking life by storm.

When you look at life through a full lens you can see the dominance on the planet and what gender has taken it by storm, quote on quote. With all these elements and degrees and conditions and poles true transformation is when it comes to your gender, it's most definitely a mental, and physical art, of being phenomenal.

Mastering your born gender, and mastering yourself, that must take place in the mind as a child, to know the role of what gender it was born to be, yes mastering you're born gender, is a physical and mental art and could be very successful if the gender is taught to love and accept their self and who they were born to be. Every child born should always know what gender it is from birth, not saying everyone is not perfect because we are all perfect, in our own way, that's what makes the two genders so phenomenal in this assimilation.

CHAPTER 3

The Divine All, We are One

"The Divine All" created the universe on a mental plane, and all planes exist in the male and female mind, it's created by their reality and action. The "All" gives us the power to embody the gift of life and the forces we experience, and that is facts.

Every event that happens in our life, we all should be honored to play the main role, male or female, adult, or child. We play an epic role in this modern time we dream in. Life has many mysteries but those who hear the message and answer the message master their life's true journey.

The one responsible and who has control over all your decisions is you, although modern-day society is one of the biggest influences on many decisions that are made on a daily.

These principles, without a doubt, are true and will most definitely add physical, spiritual, and emotional wealth to your life journey. This is not a one-way ticket to heaven or hell, there are no lotions or potions, no blood or flash you must eat or drink or rub on your skin, and I'm not selling lies, you don't have to buy a ticket to be saved, to have a phenomenal change the only thing you need to equip yourself with is an open mind to love yourself first, then know thyself, and most importantly to trust yourself, yes this is all you need to experience your phenomenal change on every level of your life. I know life is not always peaches and cream, and don't always appear to be phenomenal yes, that is when fear tries to negatively, direct your thoughts of losing a grip on your circumstances, but need I say there is always a way out of a negative mindset. As I have said many times, the mind is "All" and all your decisions are created right in the upper room of thought. I can feel a great change for those who are not fearful to face their true self.

Solution On A Positive Change

"The good news" is, destiny will always work for you. Here are a few solutions that can get you headed in the right direction of change.

- Stay positive and keep a clear mind from all negative actions and thoughts.
- Get to know yourself and know what is going on around you in your environment, and being

aware is very much relevant, and very beneficial, your destiny is yours, all things come from that one great source of love, and life is Destin to be fulfilled when we decide to tap into love, for all humanity, we will see a better world.

- Keep your desires and your thoughts, take them along the way of your life, the optimistic will of life, will manifest wherever you put your attention on, it will happen so don't spend your time living in fear, I would not recommend it, thoughts held in mind will produce after their own kind keep that in mind.
- Always know without a doubt everything is temporary.

Quick example; just look around at all these presidents that come and go, every four years, and what kind of change do they leave? Change is always one of the main words each president uses at the time of the election, that's all they do is use it, but know true action for world peace, and ending all bondage all over the world. That's the positive change that will let us know we have made progress until then there is no progress if we still have world bondage and that's a fact.

We all know nothing stays the same but at that moment of change, what are you going to do? and how are you going to handle it? Let's take a moment and reflect on how you have handled life. Let's go back into our memory bank that holds boxed up thoughts when we were babies and then the phenomenal change took us, from childhood, two a teenager, and now adulthood, what a change, who would have thought you would have handled it like this, and it happened so fast congratulations, many of you made it through the first, second and third stages of life.

I know you can agree you embraced it as time went so fast in your life, yes look back for a minute, and now look where you are today. Wow, what a change. Family all over the world, I am here and have been called to get you over, and through this next stage in your life, this part of your life brings phenomenal freedoms and amazing feelings of a fear-free mind and a fear-free world we all continue to journey in, we dream in, we expand in, create in every day.

I am here to broaden your horizon with these two words," Phenomenal Change, "as you can see lol, these words will be used throughout this book. This may be a trying time or may not be, often fear is the number one reason negative action manifests, but I am here to help you replace fear with the reinsurance, that change has always been in your present-day walk of life and, need I say there is nothing to fear, but fear is fearful of itself.
Your outer world is the reflection of your inner world, so have no fear because it will destroy you inside and out. Now let the sale up and let the wind blow you into your

destiny. Let's go on a journey in my experience in my phenomenal change.

I had to embody an epic journey in a divine way. I'm going to share my life events and show you how it has been present in my life and yours as well, like I stated before, it has not always been a happy moment.

Yes, some changes can and will be very trying and not a good place to be, and at times it would seem if no one on earth has ever gone through what you experiencing at that moment, and it does holds facts on some of the spectrum of life, and then, on the other hand, everyone experience some kind of crisis in their life or do they? Your experience is your experience, and your true reality and that's facts. Also, willingness with cooperation will exist in change.

CHAPTER 4

Sorrow Change

This kind of change that I'm talking about is called sorrow. This sorrow feels like it popped up out of thin air with no warning, right? This kind of change can bring about sadness, hopelessness, confusion with no sense of direction. I truly can say I know where the word "good grief" comes from—feeling of a broken heart or a despair type of feeling. On many occasions, it can get very ugly if not treated with the right care. This kind of sorrow change must be nourished in a positive light of understanding life circumstances. And yes, one thing I know for sure if you don't get the proper help, it can leave you in a fearful nature of what will I do next for the rest of your life, if not cared for in the right manner you will face fear over and over with no solution, you don't what to be asking yourself this question all your life, will I ever get past this change? Yes, you will, right?

Trust me when I say we will all have to face some kind of emotional dilemma in this timeline of life, and during that time it's best to reach out to family and loved ones and perhaps even a stranger to keep your insanity from going over the edge of life-changing circumstances. Yes, it is best to be around positive energy during this kind of dilemma. It doesn't matter how your emotional dilemma came about at this point in your life, it's about having the proper support to continue in this journey we call life. I can admit I have been there on many occasions and was very aware I needed positive support and yes, I knew being alone was not healthy for me. Or was it?

Let me share with you a few details of my dilemmas that threw me way off without a warning, not once, but back-to-back. It was like the biggest joke of my life and the universe was in on the whole act. My life turned on a road I have never been down, called Sorrow Lane. This road was like you have made a turn in life, now here comes your crash…yes into a brick wall of sorrow, and I didn't know if I will make it out alive, all I knew they had to use the jaws of life to set me free, from this kind of pain and sorrow. My dilemma blew me away and kept coming like it was a movie and no one told me I was in it.

Most of us never see bad news coming. I know I didn't, for quite a few moments in my life.

One day on October 31, 2015, I had gotten a call from a good friend of mine named Derrick Carter. He called and asked me did I see on the news about my daughter, Eniya's father. He was shot and killed. I said no to him, and he said, "You need to go and find out what happened right now."

That morning, when I rose out of bed, I felt something heavy in my spirit. I just couldn't call it. I knew something was not right. It all summed up when I got the call. When he began telling me the news, my heart broke into a thousand pieces, this was nothing I wanted to hear at any moment, for that matter and, so soon in this Man life, also in my daughter's life, right away I said with the phone in my hand, this is not fair to my daughter or him, his mother just passed weeks away from his death.

Eniya, our daughter, was heartbroken about that news. She was having a hard time dealing with the passing of her grandmother, or transitioning whichever one you want to call it, and then this news. Eniya and I were still in the healing process, taking steps to accept her grandmother's passing.

This true story and message that I am sharing with you have an epic twist, Eniya, father was just in the hospital Healing from a headshot wound a week earlier, he had been in the hospital for 30 days, prior to his transition, he was recovering from a fatal shot to the head, and steel had years ahead to get better. Something was telling me whoever done that to him really wanted his life to end the first time around he was shot, but yet he made it through that fight for his life, but yet it was not for long he would live.

That kind of change he was not ready for, or was he? the killer had an agenda to put him out of his mind for his own reason, how sad that was, the evil nature of that person and where he was in his mindset that morning, he took out this man for good, Brian was killed and that's facts.

In the short time, of Eniya's life with her dad, he introduced so much of his life and talents to her and told her so much about the world, he told her that she was going to overcome this world with her action and thoughts. The sorrow I felt for this man and my daughter, and then myself, messed me up mentally and spiritually for the moment. It was disbelief, and it was hard for me to accept this kind of change that we were faced with for the rest of our life. I was not ready at all, and neither was his family. I as a mother never planned on telling any of my children at a young age daddy is gone and never coming back, it felt like the biggest pill in the world and I had to swallow it whether I liked it or not, I had to tell her. I had to change fast for my baby girl and become supermom at that point, and it was not easy. I can still feel the anxiety from telling her that news. I had to be strong for her and it seems so unfair to tell her this news, all I could do is cry and look her in the face and see him in her face, and the words seem like it came out so slow motion, but I had to tell her.

Going back to his story, life changed so fast for him at that moment in time, I saw the change, that is. I had seen him two nights before he was killed. I was with two of my older daughters Maloura, Kaysha, and his daughter Calviann.

That night on October 29, 2015, we drove to Long Beach, California, to look for him. I was told by one of his family members that he was out of the hospital from the gunshot wound to the head he just faced, and he was out of the hospital, from what I heard about 5 days, and he was out looking for the person who done that to him.

Before I go on, need I say Brian and I were not a couple but good friends who respected each other's lives being apart, still sharing a child we both love, so finding out he was released, and out of the hospital, and was looking for clues, didn't sit right in my mind, and didn't sit well in my spirit. so, we drove down to Long Beach immediately, and at that time I was living in Los Angeles.

It was about 10:00 p.m., and I just got the news he was out looking for clues. I ended up finding him riding a bike where he lived in Long Beach. I was surprised he really was out looking around for clues and asking people questions. I pulled up on him and asked him what he was doing on that bike in his condition. Last, I saw him was in the hospital 2 weeks ago looking lifeless.

I told him; I was shocked to see him on a bicycle. His head was still wrapped up, and his injury was very visual, and we told him he needed to go home right away, he didn't need to be outside in that condition, he told us he was looking for the person who shot him and I was devastated when he said that. I asked him did he remember the incident happening, and he told me right away, I can barely remember anything, but I do remember my family.

We advised him to get rest and leave it alone, for now till all matters blow over with his health, but he insisted on telling us not to worry about him, "he said he didn't care what anybody said, he was getting down to the bottom of finding out who shot him." I felt like that was the last time I was going to see him for that reason he spoke on… and it was….

The guilt I felt when I got that phone call was all too real. That night, I wish I would have made Brian get in the car, but we couldn't make him go with us, he said no. We left him there, and I will never forget his smile that night and alive, eye had to let the guilt go, but it plays in mind, truth it was my last time seeing him.

But that night we shared our last moments, that will last me a lifetime. Brian made us laugh so much, talking about the different nurses that fought over him, on who was going to bathe him. He said they were fighting over him because they had never seen a man with a package that size before unconscious, and that's what made him wake up from his coma—two women fighting over him. He said, "I didn't know either of them, I never slept with them, and they were fighting over me." He said he could hear them in his sleep and that's how he woke up from his coma.

I know it's off-topic, but we all were laughing with tears running down our faces. The way he was wording his words; he was very hilarious that night on October 29, 2015, and yet he made us laugh so much we didn't want to go, and he didn't want to stop looking for that person that hurt him in such a horrible way. Brian had a car but that night, he was on that bike and it looked bizarre and strange seeing him on it, but he said it was easy for him to move around on the bike.

They also found him murdered on that bike. That night changed me forever, and I live with that change every day, a change I had no control over, and that is one of my many true stories. I wanted to share my life story to tell you about sorrow change. Brian was a great guy to know and did not deserve that kind of death in my eyes and heart, but that's how his story was written to end and became my story to tell, about how sorrow, looks in other people's life.

My sorrow didn't stop there, my baby girl cried for months because of his senseless death, yet sorrow was not over for me, by a long shot, 11 months later my middle daughter Kaysha D, her father was killed the same way on September 14, 2016, he was shot in the head by his neighbor as well, as Brian was shot by his neighbor come to find out.

Both Brian and Benny's neighbors were dealing with a mental and emotional frame of thought. Those two men who murdered these individuals were suffering from some type of dilemma in their lives, and most definitely they acted on impulse and obviously they needed help mentally, spiritually, and emotionally, due to the senseless killings of both individuals that were done on separate occasions.

Yes, we lost two fathers, and they had family that cared to see them around longer than what the killers had in mind.

Kaysha's dad and Eniya's dad had different lifestyles and lived in different neighborhoods, and they encountered one another, not often, but they both understood the roles they played in their daughters' lives. They respected one another when they encountered each other. As I stated before, they knew what role they played, yet their role ended in their daughters' lives due to the senseless killings.

What put a spin on Benny, Kaysha, father death, Kaysha and I went to look for him by his house we last knew of.

Little did we know, he had moved and stayed right down the street from his old apartment. We didn't know at that moment, but later that next day, we found out where he lived, due to the news of his death.

Kaysha had not seen her father in two years, on the other hand, I saw him out shopping with his family, one year prior to the incident.

What made life puzzling and very ironic for us, Kaysha asked September 13th, 2016, "mom can we go by my dad's house". She wanted to let him know she had made him a granddad, but we learned he had moved out so we could not find him that day. We even drove around looking for him, but we could not find him at all. I drove past his house quite a few times and didn't know he was still in the same neighborhood. At moments in my life, I can't help but think if we could have slowed the process down of anything happening to him had we gotten the good news to him about being a grandfather that day, and just maybe, it would have rewritten a new chapter for him instead of the one that ended for Benny.

Here is another ironic change we never saw coming. Kaysha's son was born on Eniya's father's birthday, July 27. Only in this matrix this would be a coincidence. I learned in this assimilation you can celebrate one life being born and a life that was being mourned because it was taken away. There again you will run into the principle of correspondence, a life is given and a life taking away in such violence.

My life story and this message are all too real, this is my true experience, getting back to the story the day I got the call once again from the same guy was kind of eerie for me, when I looked, at the caller ID, and seen who it was, it took me right back into my boxed-up memory bank about the call I got from him last, about Eniya father, I took a deep breath and swallowed when I said hello. This time he was talking before I answered the phone. I could hear him calling my name Gloria over and over, and I yelled, what with a phrenic.

He was yelling and asked if I was looking at the news. I told him, "No." Then, he said, "Turn to Channel 5 news station." The news was reporting a man being shot by his neighbor on Market Street, in Long Beach, California, on September 14, 2016. They said his name. The victim was Benny James Caesar. It was being reported, "Shot close range in the head by his neighbor due to a dispute between Benny's girlfriend and their neighbor that escalated when Benny came home from work. It ended in his senseless killing." They also were reported the girlfriend was shot multiple times and survived and was in stable condition in the hospital.

My mind was racing, and my heart was pounding hard at that moment. I dropped the phone and said, "Not again." I was very puzzled and surprised it was on the news. The news was reporting live. I couldn't believe I was experiencing this emotional change once again and so quickly down the timeline of my life. I had sobbed all the way down to the floor with such grief and sorrow from this news.

I was laying on the floor covered in tears, thoughts changing in my head on how I was going to deal with this sorrow.

I was asking myself questions: How could three men that I was involved with were killed in such a way; not once, but three times. And the same man, Derrick Carter, called me twice with the news of my daughters' fathers. That was ironic and very bizarre; it left me in a place of…I must wake up because this was the hand that I was dealt in this lifetime and it was my true reality.

My life was changed forever. I was clueless as to why it was adding up this way. And yes, there was a clear message, and I needed to receive it and I did. Reality had let me know, life is most definitely temporary and the choices we make made all the difference.

I truly can say I was devastated, because I had spoken into the universe months before saying to myself, I wouldn't want to hear of my children's father being killed in such a way ever again and yet it still happened and changed followed with my reality.

I felt so guilty about seeing Brian that night, and not forcing him to get in the car, but this time I didn't get a chance to see Ben at all, not even when we went to go look for him the day before he was killed. Life was very ironic, and I knew life was not what I thought it was but turn into an experience of mental consciousness for myself, the truth was revealed to me in reality, and the reality I was faced with was no joke.

This world and the state of its condition taught me life existed as an opposed, idealistic, realistic reality, only existing in the state of mind in this lifetime, in other words, the quality of life is a frequency that exists on many levels of life and the people you are involved with are often, on different frequencies, also on different levels mentally, physically, and spiritually. Yes, what I'm saying is that my phenomenal change happened at that very moment, receiving sorrowful news once again in my life.

Although I was not involved with either one of them, I was involved with Franklin Bridges when I received the first call about Eniya's father being killed. I was dating Franklin Bridges, and he was set up and killed by a longtime friend, someone closer than a neighbor. Yes, you read it right…another man. I know many of you may already be questioning what kind of men was this lady involved with? What I can tell you is, these men would have never done what was afflicted on them. What I can also say is that I've known and witnessed hard-working men dedicating their lives to their families, creating, expanding, and exploring the value of life; that's what I witness with each of them.

Any other lifestyle that they lived, I knew nothing about, which is why I had to write about my experience with sorrow, and share the universal message that as individuals we need to have a "phenomenal change" in this lifetime.

I questioned my reality, and once upon a time was looked at from a new point of view in my life.

Getting back to Frank's story. Frank was killed May 11, 2016, receiving the news on the evening news media, about Frank, I was very upset, in such disbelief, later that day, I found out it had made it on Facebook as well.

I knew Frank in such a short time less than one year, but we had hit it off and were really into one another ideals and plans for the present. Frank was an entrepreneur and showed not only me but many others how to start your own business. He showed and shared many talents and trades of many arts. One of his messages he spoke on believing in yourself, or thyself, nothing but fear is fearful of itself, is what he always said, if you're going to do it, don't just talk about it be about it, he said he used those phrases in his life to keep his dreams a living reality. Frank owned a few businesses that I knew of, three different apartment complexes that I visited with him on many occasions. And I met with many of his business partners all of them had successful businesses in downtown Los Angeles, California, and throughout Los Angeles County.

It was a pleasure meeting these men and women through Frank at that time and moment of my life. Most definitely they all were a part of my phenomenal change, but this kind of sorrow hurt my heart; indeed, it did.

The same day on May 11, 2016, Frank came by my house, I was picking my children up from school at that moment, he told me he was outside of my house and wanted to see me, he asked me to take a ride with him. I was surprised because I hadn't seen him in a couple of weeks, due to our busy schedule. It was not a problem for either of us, because we would talk almost every week. As I was saying, I was picking up the children from school.

Life for me had turned into a book, a story I had to write about. This sorrow change I was experiencing felt like a nightmare, a place I would rather wake up from, but that was the reality I was faced with. I was carrying emotional baggage, and I had to endure for a while. I was emotionally torn up, and fear, guilt, depression, worry, hatred is all I could feel at that moment in my life. I felt very puzzled about life and why were men dropping left and right in my circle. And especially the way the three men were killed, all in some type of pattern, it made me look at life differently. I had to change, and I had to realize life was a true journey and the principle of " cause and effect", found me with feelings of such despair, my life changed in a circle of 360 degrees; the chain of reasoning, and cause and effect, was very present, and I knew how change felt, and I knew how it felt, to never see someone that helped, shape my reality on different levels, all three men, were not related that passed away, but in fact were lovers I encountered, along the way of my life journey. My life isn't the same and literally, I could feel it, those three men were not the only men that were transitioning in my circle at that time, the other men that transitioned in my life, to name a few men that passed away back-to-back who were my relatives:

Casey Lockhart, November the 14, 2015
Alzada Morgan, Rowan, September 21, 2016
Arthur Lockhart, January 17, 2017
Lonnie Lawrence Daniels, May 11, 2018
Pastor Edward Robinson, June 10, 2018
Cliff Daniels, September 8, 2018

These men were all phenomenal men and knowing them was such an honor in every way that I knew each one of them. Knowing in my heart that I will never see them again physically makes life change and brings more respect to myself and others, and reality is a whole new understanding on an epic level. Reality shows I will never see my family that passed on, again on this plane, only in spirit, we will communicate and continue. Infinity and beyond have a whole new understanding, mentally, physically, and emotionally. Never take life for granted, for each day counts, and each one of us serves his or her purpose. Everything exists for a reason and when your body's time clock is over, no matter how you lived your life, good or bad, these vehicles; these fleshly bodies expire whether we like it or not. Transformation takes place into a higher self of consciousness.

What the body goes through doing transformation is all too real. Transforming back into pure energy is a divine process. I truly get the full spectrum about the crossroads at the end of your life. I truly can say this is a hell of a world, and we are just passing through it. Phenomenal changes, facing this journey in life, put me in a place of evolving, and I am reminded that each passing day is the opportunity to be phenomenal, mentally, physically, spiritually, and emotionally on this plane.

Mastering your emotions is much needed, also rewarding. You will feel the change right away. I see reality in time and space and the form of matter, very EPIC, in every way, that it exists only in this simulation, and much more beyond this dimension. I know, as I grow and expand my conscience thoughts, truth still is and forever will be existing in this universe. This is something all of us must face someday, truth on an epic scale.

Truthfully, I can say right now, life has so much to show you. I knew growing up life had a lot of mysteries in this world. I knew I would experience my own journey, and no doubt I did. I learned change is the only thing that is infinite and Endless and moves without measure. Change is always limitless without end.

Change makes its own space and fills up its own space; it's always in action. That's why I had to share some of my life stories with you to get you to see what sorrow change can be in other people's lives, on an epic scale. I give thanks to every one of you for being so understanding of my healing process. These are some of the steps I had to take to achieve my healing.

I know my audience didn't expect this kind of point of view, but everyone's story is different, and this message is only going in One Direction.

Never think you are the only one who has felt this kind of pain from losing a loved one. It's part of the rhythm that brings forth the vibration we experience. Time after time, we will all face change, but sorrow is one of the hardest changes of them all...

The good news is you can overcome grief at any moment of your life. The change is up to you.

I know you all can agree that sorrow comes on many levels and this message is on the level of open your mind to accept your healing from an alchemy point of view. Transformation, and transitions are not just about death, but also changing the here and now. Some attributes I am going to share with you here are some of the symptoms that cause people to feel sorrow from life dilemmas. Many people told me what they felt when they were faced with sorrow and had to change for these reasons I'm about to shed light on.

This is what sorrow looks like to others. Once again, please keep an open mind. There are many people on different levels mentally, emotionally, spiritually…yes, on different frequencies, and in a different state of mind.
This may not apply to you and may apply to someone else; these are facts and truth others have felt, expressed, and experienced.

*Unwanted pregnancy
*Unwanted marriage
*Separation/ divorce
*Child abuse
*Child abduction/adult abduction
*Can't give birth to children.
*Can't get married/ haven't found the right one?
*Teenage pregnancy/ forced abortion.
*Sterilized
*Sexual abuse/ abusive relationship
*Physical abuse/ mental abuse
*Drug abuse/ alcohol/ prescription
*Diagnosed with chronic disease/ infection.
*Placed in hospital/ nursing home.
*Incarceration/ bondage/ held without your own will.
*Learning this matrix is real.

*Transitioning/ death/ animals/ pets
*Lost home/ business/ homeless
*No food/ no clothing
*No money for long periods of time
*No career/no job/ no vision
*Fired from a job/ career/ lost business deal.
*Envy/ jealousy/ strife
*Lied on/humiliated.
*Feelings of no support
*Feeling helpless.
* Racial tensions

This list could go on and on. We all know I don't need to keep writing about the different conditions many people in the world face, we all get the picture, when it comes to the view on sorrow change.

Here are a few quick realities, Admit/recognize.

Accepting Reality

- To change, first you must admit and then recognize that you are in a sorrow state of mind.
- The second reality is to seek help right away.
- The third reality is accepting the change and moving in the direction of healing. Moving forward as soon as possible makes all the difference right away, but others may take longer in this healing process, but give them the space

they need, but keep the process going into having a brighter, and better, and healthier days and lifestyle to come.

I'm excited I got the opportunity to share this message. There is no turning back once you have started the healing process.

As I stated before, we are changing and expanding in this universe every day, and very rapidly, so it's best to start the process now. yes, it's an honor to reach out and help millions of people to awaken from sorrow changes and dilemmas, and when you come to realize you are one of the millions of people that need to heal from sorrow, that means you have crossed over into infinite change for the better.

Now this sorrow chapter has come to an end, and now we're going to move on, we must know life has so much to offer, then being sad and helpless, I know we can all agree, but you will be surprised, how many people have made this mindset a permanent lifestyle, to stay in sorrow. As we realize that we can change with grace, peace, joy, harmony, balance, reciprocity, justice, order, yes, we need all those attributes to go through this physical metamorphosis and mental change. We must accept and learn nothing stays the same. Everything vibrates and moves. We must also accept the fact that everything happens for a reason in this assimilation.

As you dive deeper, realizing phenomenal change is needed, yes it will, take your subconscious mind, to new levels of thoughts and in there, you will find out, the sky is the limit, but you are limitless my friend limitless, there is no limit on understanding change.

Once you become aware that you oversee your life-changing situations, your journey gets much easier to pursue, and yes, everyone has the right to pursue happiness.

CHAPTER 5

Social Change

Change comes along with choices and decisions that you can make at that moment of making a decision, as soon as you recognize you have the power to change, your thoughts on how you perceive everything around you, you begin to change emotionally, physically, and socially. Using your conscience to guide you out of darkness is very important. We all know the mind is All. You can do nothing without it in this simulation. I like this old phrase the elders used to speak when I was growing up, they would say" the mind is a terrible thing to waste," looking down the timeline of this life of mine, I can say that is, totally a fact. When you begin to open your subconscious mind, your divine magic opens a powerhouse of awareness on a frequency level of 360-degree awareness and/432 degrees of universal knowledge and rhythm. And no one should never perish for the lack of knowledge, if the knowledge is properly given to the people without deception, truly the people would honestly and openly know the power is truly within, we wouldn't have world chaos right now as we witness it unfold day by day here in 2020/2021. I know soon as you take full control, your behavior opens up like a Lotus flower that blossoms every day with new thoughts and actions manifesting. Your social life also plays a great role in your phenomenal change.

Being around other people with a great, and positive attitude brings so much great wealth, and health to your change, although our social behavior is shaped by trials, and tribulations, better known as the social influence, environment, authorities, economics, culture, and let me not forget politics, all play a major role, on the mass majority of people choices, and decisions today. Time, place, and situations changes along the way of this journey therefore we must keep in mind we all play a role in this social universe.

Social Change cannot be taken lightly. Now we are going to move on to another phenomenal change we all face called" Social change."

When people are made more aware of social norms, the behavior changes to become closer to that norm. That is why it is so important to have the right kind of circle, around you, 360 days of your life if possible. People always told me this phrase "birds of a feather flock together." I was told people of the same religious groups, and same beliefs on all measures run together, with people who believe in the same practices as they do good or bad, this phrase went, "getting in where you can fit in," and then it becomes a personal conflict if not careful. and it did.

I truly believe and know all humanity can change, for the better, so we can work together on making this planet a happier place to live." Social change" is a phenomenal action. It's great to be a big influence, positively on others, it's important to keep that in mind how you, value other's life, for the good of humanity, yes, it is very important to set a good example amongst your peers. Social change is a psychological term, it is defined as an alteration structure of a social group or society.

Social conflicts are always to be avoided! there is only one way you should want to treat anyone, you come in contact with, and that's treating them as you want to be treated, respectfully and indecently, globally and universal, why would you want to treat anyone other than how you respect yourself, yes I encourage you to respect yourself, and respecting someone else's freedom and will to live, otherwise, you create negative energy for personal conflict, and that brings the wrong message and negative energy to the universe and those around.

Social change is also very challenging for many, on all levels in life, it's not just social change in high school, college, job, with your neighbors, family, and friends…. etc.

Social change also stems from communist issues, like war, religion, ethnic tensions, competition for resources, and the list could go on and on. Here is a prime example of social change, as the year 2012/ 2020 rolled in, we were and still are faced with, words, like "social distance", these two words are a conflict, how can you be social, and distant at the same time, to be social, you must have a group setting, gathering of individuals, coming together to be social. Social and distance are two opposites, distance is to be set apart from something or someone, space between two things, or people, so there is no social involved in the distance. I would like to know what brains created that phrase? My point is socially, we didn't ask for certain changes, it was forced on us, in the form of a "virus" to the point wearing a face mask is becoming a mandate, but it's not the law, or in the constitution, but becoming normal. We are being changed, on a very epic level globally, without any warning. Governments, and legislation, want this to be the new normal, the new mindset for the American people.

New and normal those two words also hold a conflict, New and Normal, how can it be normal when it just got here to be new, and how can it be new if it's normal. Normal means "regular" and if normal is regular, how can something be new in something that has been regular all this time?

Some phrases don't make sense, some do more damage than good like this one, this is facts it's simply a change, we didn't ask for, also I think we could have been told the truth, why the world is changing so rapidly, this has nothing to do with a physical virus, but more, a mental virus a mindset that is controlled and conquered.

I believe we all can co-create together to make this world a better place. The elite had their own executive agenda and went at it, in a whole different direction, keeping the public in fear and clueless to the real agenda that is going forward all over the globe. This was a social change that was forced on humanity, to stay separated globally, it's happening more frequently because the race is on to build the fastest AI technology systems, that will take us into our present and future. Other countries like China and others have already identified each person, with a chip, of the cell phone, car keys, A.I. has downloaded all their whereabouts and information wherever they go, or whatever they do is recorded, that is the goal also for the United States, but very late coming into the technology world.

It's all because the silent generation and the baby boomer generation made the choice to ship all the American jobs overseas, the other countries, took the technology industry by storm and created millions of jobs, factories, and technology on a very epic scale for their economic wealth, and their generation has become faster and smarter and very talented and let me not forget clever when it comes to technology.

Our generations in America have missed out on technology that could have created great wealth for Americans, if only they would have been, giving the proper tools to do so. The X generation, and the Xennials generation, would have benefited, and could have helped, the growth and building up America, in such a way, also we wouldn't have to worry about, being so far behind in technology today.

Right now, the average American must wait on any technology to come out, they have to wait to buy, each time someone buys something overseas someone else gets rich, overseas, and not an America, he is the consumer, and that's a fact when the opportunity could have been right here in America.

This is a social and economic change, that didn't need to take place at all, now the American people must deal with a change, that is very left-wing, and right-wing, instead of dealing with the whole, double-headed eagle, that is… The average American is clueless about this kind of social change, and will never know why, so many lies, and lives, had to be, genocide, lost, destroyed, during this pandemic, America must keep up globally, and depopulation and mental illusion was few of the choices that were made on humanity.

American elites are going through a desperate change to keep up with the rest of the advanced countries.

As we set by daily and watch the local news, desperate change that is needed in the economy is proven every day on the news. What is happening right now is a prime example of why we are in this condition and why the economy is crashing, because America is trying to advance in small numbers and playing catch up in the technology world.

Now the competition is broad and America is playing catch up. Now, every day some type of change is on the News, we the people are being told bad, news like it's the norm, like this virus, that caused a great rhythm that is beyond low and very low-down. The Virus was designed to kill you physically, spiritually, and emotionally. Any plans you have in this life, in fact, it's been proven just look at the change in the body count globally due to this pandemic each day.

This economy is a philosophical, social, political, economic, ideology, movement that has been around for many decades, and their ultimate goal is to establish, a communist society, what they are telling you the agenda is, all about social economics, ordered with the structure-based, upon the ideas of common, ownership, of humans, and the means, of all production in the USA, and they also work on the absence, of a certain social class, so it can be abolished, in all honesty and truth all this separation and ownership of human lives, leads to nothing but greed and destruction.

In this system there are two major social classes; that conflict between the two classes, the ones that want it all, and the ones not getting anything at all, those are the two classes the rich and the poor. Both classes create a problem in society, and the situation will be resolved, through a social revolution, so says, Wikipedia.

As I mentioned before, the conflict is a personal agenda, and all actions first start in the upper room of thought, that's where your conflict begins, and that's where you should deal with it right there, yes to the end of your life, use your mental to make the best decisions in life, in your thoughts and actions. Anyone with the intentions and agenda to destroy someone else's life has fallen away and out of touch with reality and needs to seek out the proper help right away, for all their emotions, physically, mentally, spiritually.

It takes a lot of energy, to put an agenda together to destroy someone or billions of people's lives, and if you have plans like that, I advise you to seek mental help most definitely, right away, before another fatal decision is made.

What kind of energy does it take to

sit up and create destruction? To sit and plot other people's death all day?

One of the old phrases goes, "so without, and so within, well, as within, refers to the mind and the soul, as without, refers to the world outside the individual. I know that to be facts. You are what you think, so if a person set all day, for years focused on one agenda, you could imagine what kind of destruction that creates, internally and externally not just for that person, but other people's lives as well.

The good news is to achieve the full purpose of without, and within, you first must achieve harmony, between spiritual and mental, between the mind and the heart. The unity must take place their first, within with those attributes I just mentioned.

On the other hand. All I can do for a mindset that is mentally defeated negatively, and truly knows that is their state of condition. I must and continue to know there is always a way out and encourage better days to come if they know they need help right now. Yes, out of a dark negative place that is a waste of time for all of humanity, there is no growth there or possibility not with a mindset like that it will destroy you internally and externally.

I can only see you positively well, and completely whole emotionally, mentally, physically, and spiritually, I will keep that vision in front of all humanity globally, that's what real social change is all about, knowing that everyone matters, "WE ALL COUNT."

We are all creating this world with one mind of infinite conscience expressing ourselves, individually bringing, about a phenomenal and social change in the world.

There are no potions, no lotions, witchcraft, rituals, illusions, black magic, white magic, none, no spells, I don't have to drink blood or pretend to drink blood, I am not under any spells, it's just free will, to know your truth, and your experience, it's yours, to evolve, and love, to love yourself as you love the world, as an equal human being, exploring all possibilities in this lifetime.

The Story On Social Change

This message is enlightenment that's for sure to know when it comes to social change. It's very phenomenal if you view it in a positive and embracing way. In this part of the message, I'm going to ask you some questions, like do you remember when you were a teenager? Yes, go into your memory bank. We all have one it's written in your DNA. Do you remember your parents or loved ones that told you all about the rundown on making the wrong choices in life? Seriously think about the question, can you remember? I know we all had someone tell us about socially getting involved with the wrong crowd, or getting involved with the wrong people or person. These choices made all the difference in life. If you made the wrong move or the right move, it could lead to a lifetime of regret or on the positive, it could be a phenomenal change. When you were growing up you know somewhere along the timeline of life you needed, to make the right choices, think about that right now, what were the right choices?

You most definitely can see them in your memory bank. Many of us didn't make good choices you can see and feel what happened, were wrong directions and decisions, led to a bad outcome, and bad outcomes, always present themselves with no delay, and you have no choice but to learn from your mistakes, right?

I know at this moment you can see how far you have grown in all areas of your life. I'm going to share with you a few of the social changes I had to experience as I grow up, it was a big deal at the time, but looking back today it wasn't a big deal, I gave a lot of circumstances, and situation the power to keep me in a fearful mindset. So consciously knowing, for myself because I lived it and made it out my youth years alive, still, with the right message in my heart: love thyself and love others.

When I was growing up, I didn't know my physical body had changed yet, it didn't cross my mind that I was developing. I did not view myself as a growing, young lady, but people around me did witness my change, my physical change that is, in fact, I look grown by the body, but only 12 years old and still considered a baby, too many of my family members.

How many people know young people, that look like they are grown before their age? But we all new age can catch up to the body later down the line, male and female. I was not aware of my puberty, in fact, I never heard that word before puberty, so I didn't know my body was changing, consciously and physically, it came so fast, in my mind, I was a child, but my outer appearance said differently. All I know is I was too busy being a kid at heart, like all children have the right to do so.

I didn't know I was changing from a child to becoming a teenager so fast. I wasn't looking for it at all. Funny now, because I really didn't give it a thought it was fun being a kid 100%. I can honestly say I enjoyed my childhood. It wasn't only my environment that changed, but my body as well. I was a long-leg kid with puberty all over my body.

At that time in my life, I focused on school, but I looked forward to getting out of school at the end of the day, going home, and having a parade. That was my life, my focus. I was known as the parade girl in Long Beach, California, who rolled around in the summer inviting other kids to come out and play roller skate parade, and it was fun. Rolling around the block, over and over, it was fun. It would be days where there would be up to 40 to 50 kids having the time of their life. I was always in front of the whole pack of kids, singing, and some kids even had drums and maracas and musical flutes.

Phenomenal Change

Many parents in the neighborhood said they have never seen a skate parade. And all the parents were okay with the children rolling around on the roller skates. The parents knew the children would pass their house riding on roller skates, so there was no trouble.

I remember one parent told my mother, I was a natural-born genius to think of a skate parade that kept all the kids in harmony, no children were getting in trouble for two summers in a row, in that neighborhood back in the late 80s, and it was all about fun.

I told all the children that played with me they had to agree to just have fun, no fights, no arguments, or you could not roll with us and these kids that did get along. We were from all different ethnic backgrounds, and we socially merge, know BS or conflict, was and still are not allowed in my personal circle, for what and why? I enjoyed Bing as a kid, and I enjoy seeing other children happy just as well.

I know many will wonder what this has to do with social change growing up, well society has a lot to do with social change, society plays an epic role in your social change's as you grow and view the world, the year you were born, where you lived, and who your parents were, and your DNA, background, it all made the difference in your phenomenal walk of life. We all go through changes throughout our life, everything comes in stages.

One day I looked in the mirror at 12 years of age, and recognized I had breasts, that looked like they popped up overnight, it seems to me, like my body was on a time clock, and they were done cooking, "pop you got muffins" hot and fresh. I looked long and hard at myself and said how did I grow up so fast, I thought, I still was being looked at like a kid, but I had to realize, kids don't wear B-CUP bra size, I laughed and cried to myself, for a while, I became conscious, knowing my body was developed, and I no longer was a child, but I was very nervous, about having a mature body. I most definitely looked like a teenager, that I was for sure. That morning, when I got up for school and headed out the door on my way to school a few boys I have noticed, around in the community, and at school, but, funny they never said anything to me before, they always stared when I walk by, but that day one of them said, "Hey, one of my friends said he likes you," and a few of his other friends laughed, and I noticed one of them from last spring in the neighborhood, and our encounter wasn't pleasant.

They all stood there with no denial on their faces. They all like me, but I knew them boys were no joke. I knew not to respond to their level. Their eyes said enough. I was still on a different level mentally, although I was innocent, and Virgin to the ears, eyes, whole body for that matter, but it was all about the "change," that took place with me.

They were saying things to me I never even heard before. When I was passing by, I hurried along to make sure I got to school. I ignored the boys teasing me, but by the end of the day, my curiosity and my conscious, went from elementary to junior high graduating out of high school that day, when it came to explicit language and sexual advantages like never.

I was in a new world and conscious. I really found out in middle school also, known as junior high school, there is a different kind of mindset all young people have when they are in a social environment, like at school institutions, especially without your parents, 8 to 9 hours a day. Yes, they are in different worlds, mentally, physically, spiritually, emotionally at school, other than when you are at home.

Yes, you are different when you are with your parents, family, and loved ones, that's a fact because they truly love you personally. Public schools and private schools have proven to be a real social engineering process and a very epic place to be without your loved one's real support. In many school settings, some teachers will teach you more than curriculum.

I encountered many teachers, male and female, that were not there to teach but rather teach you sex one on one for their pleasure. Although it's not supposed to be that way, it happens more often than most parents would ever come to know.

My first sexual encounter happened at school, with a male teacher, without my consent. Yes, you read it right, I lost my virginity, and I was truly innocent at the school-on-school campus. This teacher's actions, and decided to violate the school system and my innocence, became a high-profile case in Long Beach, California, in 1989, before the end of the school year was out. I was overwhelmed, cause my mental physical and spiritual, changed earlier that spring, and very rapidly with no hesitation, experiencing life unwanted circumstances at school, done by one of the teachers in the public school system. This became one of my true experiences and my story to tell, what I experience in a social environment inside the public school system.

I always thought you could trust the school system, and your teachers when I was a child but, I was wrong, that attack from that teacher showed me different, at 12 years old. I experience much more in middle school and it changed me for all the wrong and right reasons that year. Newspapers and media coverage held no delay about my story, yes, my story hit newspapers stands in Los Angeles County, about a female student being raped by a teacher was all too real.

That spring year rolled in, it was the year 1989, and I was very clueless about the change of puberty. I felt like the girl in the movie *Carrie*. I knew I wasn't a child anymore, and why my mother didn't tell me lol.

If you can recall the movie *Carrie*, the scene when she was at school taking a shower in the girl's locker room and all of a sudden, she was not clueless anymore when it came to nature taking its natural place inside of her making her a woman, and it was very unpleasant to Carrie, to find out a woman has a cycle that causes her to have a menstrual, or period, on a monthly, she also found out she could create another life with her body, and she was still teased and made fun of because she was clueless to that experience and knowledge about the cycle of a woman.

Like Carrie when she got home, she asked her mother, why you didn't tell me about the woman's body. I, as well, was very upset. I had to learn these words from other teenagers, and adults, they used this language on a daily. I was clueless for sure and did not know teachers could use explicit language.

I didn't know what most of the words I heard meant at all, but there was no turning back from what I learned. The engineering was very epic at school, the social change took place, and from that day forward that little girl that I once knew was no more. I saw her leave in March 1989, that was the last time I saw her. She was very innocent and peer at heart. I will never forget her she was the beginning of my world, to know what gender I am, and born to be, I was everything, a little girl was born to be, without any permission, I ruled that little girl because I am her, and it was my divine living right, to be just an innocent little girl, as I was.

I was not mentally ready for the next change, but puberty was. It really hit my body like a pack of biscuits exploded everywhere on my body. In the first semester of junior high, I was developing rapidly. I often laugh about it and say it must have been all the hormones in the milk they gave us at school. Physically, I rapidly developed in junior high. I ate breakfast and launch at school, made by the school district. It had me developing rapidly from all the hormones. I still feel the school food had some part, in the changes of many youths, that develop rapidly in the 80s.

I was still innocent in my heart but more develop physically and not aware enough at that moment on my timeline of life. I knew I had to be careful of who I let in my circle. Already because of what I experienced in the spring of 1989, I made sure I picked people I wanted to get involved with. I always knew I didn't want to disappoint my mother, not including all the auntie, uncles, grandparents, and church family. They all were watching me. That was a good experience for me.

I grew up with many overseers as I look back at my memory bank. I can truly say I'm grateful for that. Although I didn't want to disappoint any of my family members, I still ran into trouble very early in my life. By the third semester I lost my virginity and by the fourth semester, I was a "Teen Mom" without my consent. The twist to that story, I lost my virginity on the school campus. I learned every teacher wasn't there to teach, some teachers were teaching more than classwork and that's facts.... I wasn't aware I was pregnant until my third trimester of pregnancy, only because I was truly too innocent to know what pregnancy felt like, and my body had not changed yet and when it did it only change 45% in my first pregnancy.

The reason why I was not aware I was pregnant was that I was very athletic. I participated in lots of school activities and sports. My body remains the same, very alkaline, and I gained hardly any weight. I was in my third trimester of pregnancy. It was a miracle the fetus survived. That long without me knowing, he was there. Those dilemmas in my young life were all about my social experience, a change that was all too real. This was another chapter in my life that I lived, and have lived beyond those experiences, of social changes in youth. I now write my own stories.

When I look back at all the girls I was around, in the early 90s, there were many sexually involved, doing drugs or alcohol, and some were hard-working, and doing positive things as well and I was still acting like a big kid, with my cousins, and the neighborhood children. I didn't want to grow up and make the wrong choices, but life circumstances still caught me by the foot. No doubt my social world around me was far more advance in sexual knowledge.

I was late and on time at the same time to learn about the talk of sex. It had already begun for many teens around me.

I found out from other girls and boys ages 9 through 18, and adults, they were already sexually involved. I was blown away, how early in life children were being curious, and yes epic number of children were sexually victimized. All kinds of stories were told to me, at many counseling centers, I attended, where most stories were told to me, during the time of my dilemma, I attend counseling because of the attack I received that spring in 1989, Its, an experience I will never forget.

All I wanted to do was roller skate and have kid fun back then, but my mother and aunt told me my body was getting too big, and people were watching me negatively ride on my roller skates, she told me, to make sure, I paid attention to my surroundings, you never know if someone is watching you, facts show in my life the statement, was true I was being preyed upon.

People are always watching someone or something, that's just the way social change happens, people watching other people and then coming up with their own thoughts and actions, and it brings about change right then and there. Becoming a teen mother wasn't my choice. Someone decided they wanted to make that choice for me. In someone else thoughts and actions, their thoughts were to have me without self-control, in their mind, then actions took control. It made me lose my virginity, something I really didn't know much about. It wasn't discussed in our family.

But many teenagers told me they lost their virginity, and some even bragged about it male and female, and not all stories warrant pleasant stories to hear, but I was curious, and I wanted to know what I didn't know, but learned quickly I didn't want to be involved, with what I have learned. Once I was aware, I knew making the wrong move could last a lifetime. This is my social change growing up, one of my example stories on how we change, and getting past those fears, of you growing up, the so-called growing pains I faced, and I made it. Or should I say to some of you we made it through a phenomenal change? How remarkable is that?

I am going to share with you some of the fears, but all young people, go through, between the ages, 9 and 18 this is also known as peer pressure.

*Being smart.
*Being popular.
* Having friends.
*Wearing nice gear/ brand clothing.
*Having a car.

*Having good hygiene/facial appearance/skin appearance.

*Making good grades.

*Passing school's test exams.

*Becoming a Teen Mom/Dad

*Gain banging

*Going to jail.

*Not getting along with teachers.

*Following rules/ at home or school and public.

*Experiencing drugs, dealing drugs, alcohol, cigarette cartridge/addictions.

*Being bullied/ made fun of

*Being forced to do things you don't want to do.

*Fearful of making the wrong choices.

I must admit most peer pressure came right out of school, that experience was very important to my social life, on making the right, and wrong decisions, it made me pay attention to my surroundings, and be aware of my life, after all, I learned most of my drama came in my youth years, in the school public system. Although I experienced motherhood at such a young age, many of those life-changing situations directed my path in a way, where my lesson was learned, and at the same time it was much more to experience, and learn, along the way of this journey little did I know.

Creating trouble is something I never wanted for myself I always knew I didn't want to get involved, so I stayed out of social groups, but at the same time I didn't judge others that got involved on the wild side of life. As I began to see the social changes in my life, I picked the friends I wanted to see in my circle. I pick people like I pick my fruit very carefully. It has been a phenomenal difference in the way I pick my friends. Twenty years ago, I couldn't do it right. I most definitely can see the growth in the personalities that I choose to keep in my circle today. It wasn't always easy.

Social Story 2

I am going to share with you another story about the social changes I faced in my life. I am sharing with you the difference in my mind as it has matured, the mindset is not the same as yesteryears.

In February 2019, I saw a high schoolmate I went to school with. I hadn't seen her in almost 25 years, she still looked the same, as I passed by her for a moment, but at that time I was in the hallway at the hospital feeling ill, I was brought into Long beach, Memorial Medical Center, that's where I, seen my old classmate at working as a nurse.

I passed by her while another nurse was taking me into my room, before I was strolled in, we caught each other's eye contact, I saw her sitting at the station with the other nurses, although I was feeling quite ill, I still recognized her face, and I yelled out her name, not loud, because she was right there nearby, and she looked up at me and said, "oh my goodness I know her that's Gloria."

They didn't sign her to my room, but I was on the floor that she worked on. Later that evening when I was resting, she came by and visit with me, the nurses told me that the next am. They told me I had a visitor last night, and she didn't want to wake me up. I told the nurses that was so sweet for her to come by and see what was going on with me, although I didn't get a chance to speak with her or see her again at the hospital, it most definitely was a joy to know she came by. Later that day I was released from the hospital and I was thinking to myself, it sure would've, been nice to have conversated, with my old classmate, lol. In this world I have learned to be careful, for what you ask for because it can manifest and come to pass good or bad, The Mind is All. It means everything to your phenomenal experience.

A few weeks passed by, and I see the same high school classmate at another job she worked at, how ironic, I walked in at the work source office also called the GAIN office, where many people go to get help with employment, and other referrals in Long Beach Ca. I was shocked because I had just seen her, weeks ago as a nurse, so the first thing I said was, what are you doing here? laughing at the same time, she was laughing just as well, telling me I have two jobs and she was very excited talking about it, she said, I work here as a security guard, I laughed again because it was like her character as I remembered her in high school, she had to be everywhere, and in everyone business lol.

This classmate as I remember her knew everyone in our high school, and all the teachers, at that time it didn't matter what gender they were she was a social butterfly, as I would like to put it so nicely lol, or I could say she was most definitely Miss popularity. I was very popular as well. My popularity was in another form of energy. I was politically minded. I mind my own business smart and am aware of my surrounding. Yes, most of my peers knew this about me, including her. I got the nickname Oprah Winfrey from her back in high school.

She would say, "Go ask Glo, that's Oprah, she knows everything." I would be standing nearby and they would all laugh, all her crowd of friends, she would tell other students, if they needed help with homework, saying it to be sarcastic, and helpful at the same time, ask Oprah, I felt like I was being punked, so I didn't help when any of them asked me for help, lol them memories are like gold the value of it will last a lifetime.

But it was so exciting to see her again, I like seeing how we look as women versus when we were young girls like I stated before, she looks the same, just a little heavier than when we were in high school, we all know we change, as we grow up into adults, her sense of humor hadn't changed much, she was still loud talking, and very funny just like in high school. When we were in high school, she kept a crowd around. There were many girls and boys at school that kept her company she was the ringleader and always was ready to fight anyone who looked at her wrong.

Although we never fought, she took pleasure in clowning and talking about me to other girls to make them laugh when I walked by. It was many days I dreaded walking by her lol, but I always kept it cool with everyone at school. I stayed on her good side lol, I am still talking about the mindset and the social changes I had to face.

This message is to all genders and walks of life. At this time in my life, it was very trying between 10th and 12 grades, they were very difficult for me, socially, that's why I kept to myself and it helped in a good and bad way. The name of the school we attended was called "READ HIGH SCHOOL." Now, this same school is called "Renaissance Performing Arts school" in Long Beach, California. When I attended "Read high school" in 1990, you could take your child to school. The child's age could be between 6 weeks old up to 2 years of age. It helps furthered you along with your education, many young women had no excuse about dropping out. It wasn't an excuse at that school. Many young women and young men benefited from that nursery program, and I was one of them that did.

"Read High," gave you extra credit for working in the nursery. I worked fifth period, and each student had to participate, and care for the other young mothers' babies, and help the nursery staff keep the nursery clean. The young woman I'm speaking about also was a teen mom as well. Her daughter was the first baby, they had signed me too, in fifth period. She didn't know for quite some time that I was picked to be her baby helper, but when she found out, she didn't like the fact that I was picked. Although, I didn't have a problem with any baby.

One lunch period, she looked in the nursery window and saw that I was caring for her daughter. She walked in and told me in front of everyone. "I don't want you picking up my baby," and I don't know where your hands have been.

No doubt she was trying to embarrass me lol, but I cared for her daughter and any baby in the nursery all in love, as I wanted the same for my son because he was in the same nursery Bing cared for by another student. I adored her child. Her baby was one of the first babies I had ever seen so beautifully in my eyes at that moment in time. She was the true definition of the word "adorable" if there was to be a picture in the encyclopedia her baby's face should've been right there, that's how adorable she looked. She had the deepest dimples; her face was smooth and round and very chocolate. She was most definitely a living baby doll, and on top of it, she smelled exactly how a baby should smell. That baby was too cute, I thought to myself, and her mother was a bully, back in the days.

Well, getting back to the moral of the story.
I ran into her at her second job, where she worked at. That day I had my son with me, he is one of two boys I have one set of twins.

That day we entered the work source center, and when we open the doors, there was security. I looked up and seen my old classmate, sitting at the end of the security table, I had to put my items and purse through the machine so they could be scanned, to make sure there weren't any weapons, as my son and I went through the metal detective machine, everything was fine she and I were talking, as soon as we crossed over the metal detective machine, the buzzer went off. Right away she yelled, I'm going to beat up your son, the buzzer alarm was going off in the whole building, many of the workers came out to investigate the noisy alarm, it was very loud.

She was very loud and laughing and people were looking at us like he really pushed that button in my head. I heard a still voice saying she was still a bully and I was embarrassed for her. It made that situation looked bad, in front of a lot of people, the looks my son and I got were not cool, her and her security guard colleague were laughing and shaking their heads. She insisted on saying my son hit the button, but the button was on her side of the machine, where they sit to monitor the items going through the conveyor machine.

Like I said before, we just, walked in, only to stop to talk to her for a moment, before the alarm went off, her colleagues were laughing as well, because of the way she was talking to me, and I didn't find it funny, it was a discomforting feeling like, I was in high school again lol, it felt like I was being pranked and she was letting me know she was still in charge of her circle, wherever that circle may be.

Don't get me wrong, I love the dominance in a woman, but some people energy can be overbearing, some people, in this world, will go toe to toe with you, and create a chaotic scene, for myself I didn't want to bring, drama or any kind of embarrassment, into my circle it's not necessary. Well, after all the chaos, she mentioned her party and invited me to join her celebration. Soon after the drama, she asked me about it. I couldn't give a reaction or an answer, to that drama, she asked, after a moment she changed energies, quickly to invite me, after all that chaos at the front entry, I quickly made up my mind, my thoughts went right on my big project anyway, I had to work on over the weekend. I didn't have the time if I wanted to go to her birthday party, so I quickly thought in my head that those bullying days are over. The way I was treated in high school was long over. Those kinds of situations. I would not put myself in a heated situation, not in today's world, or any world for that matter. An uncomfortable feeling, NO thanks.

I would never know if I wouldn't have had a good time or not, and I was not going to find out. I had many uncomfortable situations in the past with her, and now this, and that, was enough.

I knew, what I was dealing with, she showed me actions speak louder than words, that kind of social dilemma I faced, was long over, now I pick the situations, I put myself in, and yes, in other words, I didn't want to find out so right then and there, I already made up my mind. Yes, I embrace the fact that I was a grown woman, and this was not a high school musical, or making the band, or bad Girls Club, but indeed, my true journey of life.

Now I control my own social environment and the narrative in my life's journey. A week passed, and I had to be back at the office, where my old classmate worked as a security guard, as I pulled up in the parking lot my mind began to reminisce on the incident last week, but I had the paperwork I needed to turn in, for all my services to be complete. My old classmate, her birthday party was that weekend that passed. I didn't attend, and I felt a little guilty for not going, but I was too busy working on a project, and it took up all my weekends. So, I walked into the lobby and didn't know if I would see her, because I didn't know her schedule, and yes, she was there, I walked in, and she looked me up and down, and rolled her eyes, right away, I smiled and laughed and said, hey sis, how was your birthday party?

She said very quickly, "You would have known if you had come," with a very unpleasant voice. I told her I was out of town, and she quickly said, "Stop lying," in a very nasty tone, with a look on her face like she didn't believe me.

I hit her on the arm, and said, "I know you changed; don't be like that., I love you, sis."

She smiled and said, "Ain't nothing changed about me I am still the same. I'm not rowdy anymore. I don't fight, but I still keep it real. I still speak my mind, Gloria."

I said to myself, *This is one reason why I am writing; I know we all can have a "Phenomenal Change."* I truly was blown away, with her statement, because you all know how I feel about the word "change" and she said she hasn't changed much, and I believe in everyone to have that phenomenal change, that is desperately needed, all around the world mentally, physically, spiritually and let me not forget emotionally.

I couldn't receive her statement about her, in my mind, I know different and believe in everyone phenomenal change, but because of her statement, I was saying in my head, in other words, you are saying you are still a bully, lol, she started laughing, after she made that statement, I started laughing just as well.

I felt better that we broke the ice and our laughter heal the wounds of yesteryears. Those feelings that I had boxed up for years finally had gotten tossed out that day. I should have thrown out those feelings a long time ago, but I had to face myself, and the feeling of being bullied by anyone, although I had made up my mind, last week I wasn't going to go because of that, bizarre incident, an unexpected embarrassment, because of someone else's actions, but I couldn't take that chance, having anyone attack me in that way, not saying that was going to be the case, but remember old phrases goes "birds of a feather flock together."

My social changes have been quite a journey, learning how to socialize as I journey through this world.

I have grown enough and expanded in my life enough to know what kind of energy I'm feeling when I get around certain people, and what kind of feelings I like to experience when I am in any social environment, I prefer to surround myself with greatness mentally, physically, spiritually, and emotionally. I would never choose to put myself in an embarrassing dilemma, but other people have no problem putting you in a situation or environment that you didn't plan on being in.

Many people will create environments intentionally that are negative just to see you embarrassed whether it's a birthday party or anywhere. Some people just like chaos and dirty looks and like to feel egotistical about putting you in a negative situation. No Thanks: those clowning days are over lol. My old school friend, Sierra. She told me she had a good time anyhow at her birthday party in February 2019, and I know she had a phenomenal time. I may or may not see her anymore, but she was a part of my world, my growing world, that is.

I know many thoughts and actions manifest, not knowing we magnified it, and now it has come to pass, there is a lesson, and many situations will show up but it's all how you handle it at that present moment. So, remember when I made this statement, I would have like to have seen her again and it was so, I used this story to show you my experience it may not always have been pleasant in my life, and it may not always be pleasant, in high school with friends but, I still had my phenomenal experience, and change, it took place coming out of high school," good riddance," immature energy lol.

As for my friends today not many at all, but that's a choice, I know for sure I am not the girl of yesteryears, many of our high school friends, held on to certain friendships for certain reasons, and grew together, sometimes certain dilemmas happen, that made people stay friends as well, life has its way of keeping certain people together, and that's an individual's choice.

For myself, I didn't like the influence of my friends. I was always the main one getting in trouble because I was very naïve when it came to following the crowd and trusting their path. I have seen many of my old high school friends, and college friends throughout the years, but only a few I chose to keep up with, I most definitely can see the directions each last one of us was headed in, and everyone wasn't worth following that's for sure. I always did what I thought was right. I encouraged everyone and wished them well. I am glad I didn't keep up with many of my high school friends, I believe my mindset would not be where it is today if I would have stayed in the same mind, to clown around, and think it's still ok to be disrespectful, that circle of people, is like a never-ending high school reunion, and no one grows up mentally out of the high school mentality.

I know I wouldn't have been able to move forward 360 degrees to know my true self if eye would have kept up with most of my high school friend's, other people's influence will lead you to places you never intended to go before they mentioned any of their ideas to you. Always keep that in mind. "Thoughts held in mind produce after their own kind." And too much negative influence can lead you away from your own path. I thank goodness for the positive energy that set my path to a clear vision of infinite possibility that leads me to the abundance of spiritual, and mental, wealth.

Following my own mindset let me discover myself, it gave me time to sit quietly, and think about what kind of social environment I wanted to be involved with, so I headed on a journey, working for humanity, I surrounded myself with human rights activists, and very positive, and enlightening entrepreneur women, and men, and some courageous children, who also have the mindset to co-create. I have met men and women along my path that, showed me how to talk maturity, how to talk positively and, respectfully, how to treat others when I encounter anyone, energy good or bad, I was shown the option to leave a positive impact, it's most definitely yours, what will you do at every given moment of your life, when you encounter anyone or a situation? It all makes sense to me, treat others as you will want to be treated, with the same respect.

Having positive people in your life reflects yourself, like looking in the mirror at your behavior that you tolerate positive or negative, it's an honor that I can reflect positively, Like the old phrase go" pick your friends like you pick your fruit," "we all know you wouldn't pick bad fruit, would you? It spoils the whole batch of good fruits, we know that for a fact. When it comes to social change, many of our friends can influence all areas of our life if you let them, in a negative way or perhaps, many of them are just trying to be helpful so they think, with good intentions planning your whole life, and I'm not talking about disadvantage people, who can't think for themselves, who need help.

We all can admit it is phenomenal when you have a great and positive friend or friends in your life. It's something money couldn't buy a phenomenal friend. On the other hand, some so-called friends will dictate your whole life if you let them lol. Let me explain, like these certain friends that are always directing your opinion like who you should be friends with, control the college U pick, your career, the kind of car you drive, what type of home you buy, give you the OK on your boyfriend or your husband or wife, if you should have kids and how many, how you should spend your money, or even how you make your money, this kind of influence is all around the world globally, every day by our so-called friends.

The narrative of the story is making sure the number one principle of your friendship is respect, of others reflecting positive and, great, energy that will bring about positive behavior, in your mental and spiritual character, so it may Brighton your horizon in harmony in this world, no matter who you are, or where you are in the world, bring about good friends that has good qualities that reflect positive energy and help bring out the best in you always. Here are a few positive actions and qualities you would want your friends to have, to bring about a positive experience when you are together.

- Self-Respect Righteous attitude
- Respectful attitude Honorable attitude

- Honest attitude
- Peaceful attitude
- Noble attitude
- Decent attitude
- Irreproachable attitude
- Law abiding attitude
- Loving attitude
- Joyful attitude
- Prosperous attitude

We all know the list could go on and on, you get the full picture, of a good healthy social lifestyle and attitude. As we move up the social ladder of life choices, know that choices are free, there is no charge to your credit card or your bank account, there are no hidden fees, and no overdraft accounts, your social life should not have to pay a negative price. I am on this journey to get you to see your mind is changing, your mind wants to expand, and it already has. Trust me, I know you can feel and visualize your phenomenal change.

CHAPTER 6

Times Change

Moving right along, everyone has a story to tell, and it takes a lot of courage to tell it, all in due time, right? Just think about it. Our family members can be part of our social life as well, most of them bear witness to the change in you. Some of us have completely changed, and family sees the difference in our behavior, positive or negative, many of our family influence has been the reason why, we are the way we are today, not saying our family influence wasn't the best for us, but the influence most definitely was there.

Family influence and family settings and values are needed on an epic level in this world today, we all can bear witness time has changed. Know it's not the same as it was 20, 30 years ago each generation had their own experience. Now the family structure is totally different to the point it seems Mom and Dad are not needed. The love of any stranger is more important so says society, it has become the norm it seems, but I am witnessing, more and more confused generations, lost with no real sense of direction and most don't know why they are alive that's facts.

Family influence has become very political, woman, man, and child that family is no longer the norm, although the true, Holy Trinity will always be, Man, Woman, and Child the way nature designed it... Time has changed so much it's a fight to keep the natural family together, just look at society, what is a normal family in today's world? Universal law and government law are completely different.

Universal law created the natural family, government laws have bent and stretched the laws of the land, sea, air, and natural seeds for families and crops to grow naturally. Legislation and their laws have set aside the natural family to accommodate the feelings of others and groups that only think of themselves and their alternative lifestyle whatever that may consist of, not caring about what kind of image and intentional ill-will, that will be left behind on the next generation. On the same scale, government laws and accommodations outweigh the natural way of life, and that will bring about a change. Time will only tell where we are headed. Will the natural family make it out of this simulation with all the government agenda set in motion? No doubt, secret societies have an agenda that is designed to depopulate healthy families in this 2020, 2021 pandemic.

This pandemic holds the evidence to what I'm saying today, just turn to the local news, and you will hear and see the news media talk about the change that is taking place with our elders during this pandemic.

Are people dying? Are families losing the right to be with their family at a time like this? Right now, as you read this message, can you go to your local hospital with your family member who is an elder? Go ahead and you will see for yourself.

I will ask again: Are we being separated? Are they separating families for their own good? Will the natural family, woman, man, and child be together 20 years from now on this planet will we still be a unit? Will it only be nothing but death in our future or will it be, natural life Being produced to carry on the legacy of life and family. Time has changed on many levels. The way families are scattered and separate because of so many dilemmas and unwanted circumstances, yes it all plays a role in the new family setting today. The world our family is faced with shows us the new family is based on social media and virtual reality. We all know social media is an allusion, based on no real evidence, it only appears to look one way but may not hold facts, on the other end of the virtual reality that is put before your eyes.

The truth is if you are not there in person to see your family physically change, the image and illusion can be very deceiving. Most definitely time has changed, and the process that the family is up against makes it difficult to hold on to sacred values that started this world to rolling in the first place.

I give thanks to all the families that paid it forward, to show other generations how to continue as a sacred family on this planet. It's not like when we were growing up and everyone was present in the family—mother, father, sisters, brothers, cousins, uncles, aunties, grandparents, extended family, you name it—that began one village. As we see, times have changed so much around the world, one question I ask is, is family important in today's world? Now that you are all grown up, is it important to keep family around? For your or their own personal reasoning?

Family members are the main ones to notice your change before anyone outside your family notice, because they know you on a personal level. Every birthday, accomplishment it doesn't matter, what the occasion is family shares it with you. In my family, the older generation always encouraged us to be all we can be, even though they had to experience life in stages just as well. The older generation in my family always told us how times have changed, according to how they lived, many of the older generations were baby boomers.

They also were the GI generation, and the silent generation they witness this world change so much good and bad.

I, too, watch this world fold up like origami in so many ways it may never unfold again. To see its natural beauty without a spot or wrinkle, generation after generation. I truly enjoy hearing the elders speak about the phenomenal change they lived. Phenomenal change true stories, it's not always about me telling my story, but most importantly it's up to you, to see your change and tell your story, and how you made it through your phenomenal change and stages, and yes give yourself the credit you deserve.

Once again, many of the changes you face it's not just because of you, many of our family members had to pay the price for you to be here today, positive or negative. looking back at your family tree is very much needed to see the family growth, evolution, and social change, and economic change and growth. Your family evolution and their history on this earth is important, as evidence shows how far you have come, in the knowledge, skills, awareness, and many manifestations, has already happened yes you are here right?

With all these changes that we see and hear about, most definitely the other generation before you had to experience a lot of unwanted circumstances and growing pains for you to be where you are today. Many of us came from a family line with mental, physical, and spiritual morals that helped make the difference on this journey of life. Also coming from a family of economic wealth and great assets paved the way, yes let us be real, it made your journey much more comfortable and easy selling, although family members may not be around today, you evolve because of the time they put in, and let me not forget a lot of us inherited common sense wealth, and it shows, I believe it can skip generations, but most definitely someone will benefit from their family's contribution.

Once again, does your family matter to you?

Over the course of life, it has been designed to change generation after generation. Many of our family members' environment was not like the ones we live in today.

I feel as though that's good, because on the other hand it is so much more expanding, we can do as a nation to make this world a better place, we all know that to be facts.

We still have thousands of old sacred stones and pictures, that prove time has changed, and many things were manifested already, life before us exposes they pave the way, and we bring witness to that fact every time an anthropologist pull sacred artifacts out of the ground, and it is much more to discover. The millennium generation, also known as generation(y).

Many of them have shared with me they noticed times were different. I was told by two young men from the (y) generation, who are brothers, that they were discussing how the majority of their friends are not raised by both parents. It seems Dad was not included, and many of the millennium generation didn't get the opportunity to share both parents under one household. This is because generation after generation has had their own trials and tribulation that made the experience of absent parent to be what it is today.

Studies show all over the U.S., single families have hit an all-time high of 80% of single - parent household are moms, and 25% are fathers an additional 7% live with unmarried co-parenting family members, or non-family members not by bloodline. The solution today is still the same solution decades ago. We all must make an impact on the family morals and values enter standing that what we do and say all counts. knowing this virtual, is important. Universal law helps us to recognize morals and values can bring about the best version of the sacred family today, if we simply all lived by the laws of harmony. All generations should have been shown and taught, that in this life it's about you, and knowing your history, and your family heritage and revolution is a big dill, what they made it through, it lets you know you can make it as well.

I made a phenomenal decision, and the calling was there from the beginning in my DNA blood line.

This was one of my family tree assignments for myself to impact the world, in this way, in this lifetime positively no doubt. Having a made-up mind and a positive mindset about changing your lifestyle for the better is all worth it, facts have proven all around the world, knowing your family history tells and shows they have been here, and you are still here.

The phenomenal change in our generation is very rich just look around, infinite discoveries right before your eyes on many levels discovering and unveiling this matrix. I'm going to give you another prime example. The generation we sit in today is called" generation Alpha," also known as the" I "generation." this generation is the most technological-infused, at demographics, on many epic levels. The Alpha generation has a world that is being introduced to them whether they like it or not, they did not ask for most things pushed on them, but other generations like"The last generation" and the Interbellum Generation around the 19th century had already begun, making decision long, before this generation, even knew they had a history, and a blood line, long before those generations, knew they had an obligation to society to pay it forward.

The Lost generation had to endure World War 1 and World War 2, also other battles mentally, emotionally, physically, and spiritually, along the timeline of the United States, darkest dilemmas. Most definitely decisions that were made affected their influence, economics, social environment, so laws were created to help the government, take the people by storm with all kinds of unjust laws, and long-time coming laws that needed to be passed, and many laws that never should have been a law in the first place. It all plays a major role in today's Alpha generation, that's why they are so stagnant, because the illusion looks as if there is nothing left to eat at the table.

Many of our family members in our bloodline suffered and had an unpleasant experience along the journey of life, and there is no need for repeat, many of our children will not know the history, at how they came to be, if phenomenal change doesn't take place with each individual. The interbellum generation was one of the greatest generations many say but, on the other hand the silent generation, the baby boomer generation, the Generation X, and the Xennials generation were here long before the millenniums were here and time have proven the families had to be strong and fight to stay alive just as we do today. Perhaps you are still living and have lived through all the generations I have named. This generation faced a different dilemma, in fact, they all did, and if you live through any of that, then yes, you are phenomenal. What an honor, or is it for you? Yes, you got to see each generation come and go, and you are still living. How phenomenal specially, if you made a positive influence on the family structure globally, so we all can continue to thrive today. Yes, take a moment and be proud of your accomplishments and your positive impact even if it was a small contribution it helped.

We all know there were other generations like the Golden generation, the bronze generation, the silver generation, I will not go into details about those sacred times, but they were the biggest generational influence that pave the way for the sacred family to thrive today, yes, they created, they expanded unimaginable leaving existence and evidence at every four corners of the earth showing families existed. You can do plenty of research about the sacred families all over the world, and I'm not talking about the evil and greedy groups of families that continues deceiving and destroying other countries and looting there resources not for economics but to keep a class of people, in a state of mind of a fearful and a conquered spirit, and energy that will never rise to his highest potential.

So, the generations and the offspring of sacred families witness worthless power that can't even come close to healing this sacred land and connecting with the cosmos. No real power to heal the land globally without human trafficking, and bondage happening every day what a disgrace.

These so-called elite families seem to think they are sacred because of their evil deeds and psychopathic influence that they have on society today. You can clearly see their agenda is not connected with the universal laws. The counterfeit families are not honoring the way nature naturally intended it to be, with the natural vibration that comes from the earth that achieves harmony on an epic level. Therefore, those small families hold absolutely no true illuminating powers, to do what's right for the good of all humanity globally and universal.

These counterfeit families really don't know how to achieve or understand sacred values and morals, and the true obligation to nature.

Yes, sacred families hold the keys to unlocking the universal knowledge and natural seeds that helps this world grow. At this point it is desperately needed to continue as the sacred families on this planet. Will our morals survive this state of conscience, that's on this planet right now.

To learn the history of each generation, and how we got here in America today is one of the most important reason to know thyself, native or not, your family history is an epic deal. The narrative involving the sacred family is, times have changed in your family whether you knew it or not.

Truth be told, the Millennium and all the generations under them have a world where everything pretty much can go any way. They like it, yes also with plenty of "evil dictation" if your life is not guarded. Yes, I believe and know the Millennium would have much more to offer if those worthless agendas didn't exist in the past, and if they stop creating, worthless agendas that truly stagnate the growth of humanity in this present day. These agendas that are implemented on the sacred family capture their highest potential no doubt, and most sacred families are led astray because most of the agendas are nonsense. Yes, life existence could be experiencing phenomenon after phenomenon, and experiencing higher horizon in consciousness and mobility to carry on. Instead, this generation is faced with pandemics, an addiction from social media, drugs, alcohol, sex addictions on every level mentally, and physically and let me not forget emotionally. So yes, instead you will witness and see the lack in the millenniums also known as the A.I. generation.

This is the generation that created the A. I. with all the high demand on the" NET," A.I. most definitely was created by the Millenniums. They created it with thousands of apps that hold a high demand society needs or wants. The Millennium generation put their own mark on creating apps to surf the web for their needs, this generation learned everything from each other, young people surf, the web like going to the beach every day, creating that AI, that we see today in this simulation, matrix, world, however you want to look at it's all the same. You could never tell me this generation is not the swiftest and one of the strongest generations mentally, and up for a challenge on every epic level, of have it your way however that is, and time will tell how dangerous that kind of mindset can be or won't be.

We all witness scientists of today change everything to fit governments agendas even if it's not good for the people that change is going to happen, to fit the plan how the world should be Govern, you will read or listen, to what the News says, the talk about America, on an epic scale you will learn, time will tell on itself.

Most people are not aware of the real situation we face collectively as a whole human race. I know my readers can agree we all have had a phenomenal change generation after generation with so much implemented on the people by the Interbellum Generaion. Everyone is being affected by the chaos that happened, and still happening here in the U. S. If you are native to this land, you know what I'm referring to. Also, all over the world, the USA is known for involving their self in other countries resources, the game of divide and conquer, my question is why is it necessary to conquer someone else resources on their own land?

Why would they want to divide and steel when trading and bartering is the natural and honorable way to exchange and expand? They say the last generation of the United States, dates 1900 through 1942, made most of these laws, and executive orders, they came from that generation that say they had the best years USA had ever, seen, because that is the time United States were laying the laws and their foundation completely down, between 1869 and 1877, I guess when Grant was the president, he was known for the victory over their Confederate States of America, during the American Civil War.

Also, the greatest moment in American history was in 1776, but reality also shows in the last 50 years our laws have been passed and denied like never before. But the biggest impact positively came when laws really made a difference, during the time of Generation X, between the years of, 1965-1979, they were the most influential generation of all time, they really made the phrase "Be All You Can Be", what it is today.

The X generation were very independent, very resourceful, and self-sufficient. Freedom for that generation, mentally, physically, and spiritually was there, responsibility to the world and they made a very positive impact. In today's society the Washington post says, the generation X, Millennium and generation Z have become the lowest influential generation today.

Well, I don't agree, this statement was pushed on them by the silent generation, they were not called the silent generation just to be called the silent generation, it all has a significant meaning, research the years, and find out what was going on at that time, in the matrix, and you will see for yourself. The silent generation were not silent, they had a plan, as you can see it worked, just look how the world looks today 2020/2021, it has changed, with all the laws an executive order signed by different generations of president, who had many agendas, War, and economic depression, reflected the counterculture, syndrome we face today, and still what's at the top of the list today, War against humanity what has changed?

This mindset came long before this Millennium generation could spell generations. Facts shows many discussions was made, and many meetings did happen to pass laws, fair and unfair, that's why the Millennium generation inherited a world worth of BS, mentally, physically, spiritually, emotionally, on a broad scale, this Millennium generation didn't ask for this mess, that decision was already made for them.

Yes, it's easier for other generations to blame the Millennium generation, for being lazy, but that's how it was setup over the years, they sent, all the jobs away, that could have made a major impact here in the USA, but instead those jobs went overseas, where all the wealth followed, hitting economic numbers at 13.37 trillion dollars a year, putting a 5.47 trillion-dollar GDP gap between the United States and China.

The study show in 2019 the value of this economy in terms of gpd was at 21.44 trillion, while the Chinese economy was measured at 27.31 trillion dollars not including the rest of the world economics, so yes it is easy to pass an illusion to look at this generation like they have failed the economy, and it's the other way around, they failed to be prepared for the Millennium generation to have all the necessities they needed to thrive, in this so-called New World, it sounds very contradictory in my mind. Well, this happened because many meetings that went forward without, the millenniums and other generations that needed to be there at the oval table, but instead, now all we hear is negative criticism about a generation they didn't, prepare for, and the millenniums, are bashed for not being on board with this new world.

They may have one or two options in the matrix, and you can pretty much figure out which have no place in society. This generation has been ordered to change negatively and positively worldwide, go figure, or you can take the other road, and have a phenomenal change, freeing your mind mentally, physically spiritually and emotionally and unplugging from the matrix. I have stated before we all shape this world we live in. It is up to you who you let influence your development, judgment, and values in this lifetime, so let your light shine in this world as bright as possible, and there you will see your individual power on making an impact in this lifetime, or you will be labeled good for nothing and used as such.......

It seems, it comes naturally to make hasty judgment on the future generations to come, passing judgment against other generation like the government's agendas didn't play a major influence, legislation took orders and set the bar so high, they knew other generations under generation X couldn't begin to reach the bar yet alone find a ladder that they can use, buy, rent, to reach it.

There are honest ways of living that can benefit the Millennium, but other generation lead with corrupted examples, we witness whistleblowers, every day on local news exposing the lies that haunts America. This shows the Millennium generation the only way you can reach the bar is by stepping on someone else's back, that is already down, and climb on them to get to the top, and that is the true reality in many generations. Look around at the world. What are you willing to sacrifice? Is all I hear from the elites that ruin this world, do we really need to sacrifice anything to get ahead? If so, what kind of influence and company you have encounter that requires you to take this kind of action that is so epic. This is a question you need to think long and hard about.

To reach the bar. Think about it, yes it has been made aware that right here in the good old USA, and I can see why the bar is set so high, greed has proved time and time again it won't change, US economy is no longer the world largest.

China and the European Union have produced a bigger and stronger economy putting a very large gap in there, financial wealth, I find it to be very humorous covet 19 still didn't touch China economy, as times continue to change what will happen to the USA economy with all the people out of work and unemployed at this point. The USA, has made a powerful impact on mask, yes this the biggest masquerade event in the world and everyone is invited all around the communist globe, but the business revenue in the USA it is still up and running because of all the consuming that goes on here, just think if it wasn't for the consuming the Xennials generation and the Millenniums generation does, there will be no economy to balance here in the USA, to stay in the Monopoly game that is played in the matrix with other countries. I often wonder what will become of the United States as generations go by, only time will tell, talk about phenomenal change taking place here in the entire United States, if the consciousness of the elite does what is right for all humanity there will be much more harmony to come.

I believe this United States can change for the better, also I know many other great countries know this as well. When the conscience and the heart of American elites change for the good, other countries will also see and reap the effect. There will be less resource conflict on other countries' lands, if the United States took on their own responsibility with finding the resources within their own country to continue thriving like other independent countries do. More importantly, if this action was taken here in the United States, this country wouldn't look like a charity case, bullying other countries for their resources…

I know this is a big pain pill many American Patriots must swallow, but we cannot deny this country needs a Divine and Supreme facelift, starting with pulling yourself up by the bootstraps and start building with the Americans right here on the land. The good news is the universe is always growing and has grown from the beginning of time expanding in more than one way and so can America. This change is a good change, right?

Yes, the whole world will play a part in this change, other countries know this to be true, that's why it means everything to them to hold on to their resources, and assets in order to function, effectively in this simulation on their land. The value of people, materials, money, environment, is most important, it's more profound and effective when you Co- create with the Patriots in your country, how can this country lose, when it comes to their economy, if they work together with their own people, right here on this land in the old USA. Survival and well- being will have a whole new world. Ask yourself, is it important to know what's the number one priority, in this growing country? or does it even matter, or did, USA, give up on the people and did the people give up on these systems here in the USA? this country right now is at a stand down across the whole sector of peace and harmony. It would benefit the United States of America to come together collectively to co- create and envision a whole new experience that brings about phenomenal change.

CHAPTER 7

World Change

As we continue down the process of phenomenal change, let me remind you that this change is about you, and your awareness, and how you make a difference, in this world as it changes, and you change as well. Although you may be aware or not aware the world is changing, so fast if you turn your head in one direction, you may miss what is coming in the other direction. You should keep your head on 360*. Yes, keep a positive outlook on the world around you. Always be aware, and know where you're going, as the world changes around you. I know that brilliant minds have made life a little easier to cope with, by writing books, writing music to bring about growth and change.

When I say brilliant minds, I am speaking about songwriters. They were telling us through songs that we needed to change our views. People like Kem, and his song, "Love Always Win." Kem's music is for the ages. It will always be around to send a clear message, to the world that it needs more love right now involving relationships, brilliant minds also like Sam Cooke, and his song, "A Change is Gonna Come," Marvin Gaye, songwriter/producer, put out a hit, called "What's Going On." The message was plain and simple: the world needed compassion and harmony, not a war against the American people.

These kinds of messages had to be left, and millions receive the message, about the trying times America faced and needed to have a change of heart, and many did change their worldly ways, to bring about harmony, and made a real change for the better cause for humanity. Yes, because the music did help the world to heal. As we look back, the question is still the same: what's going on and what's happening? Does anyone know what is going on in this world in 2020/2021? Also, songwriters like Billie Holiday left a message with her song, "Strange Fruit," that impacted the US. The message was clear—laws needed to change in the USA, ASAP. Should I say once again why?

Senseless murders and the smell of bodies hanging everywhere in America. Blood was boiling generation after generation, because of the chaos many had to witness along the timeline of their lives, and that birthed out many rap artists like Public Enemy that created songs like "Fight the Power." Later on down the line because of the unfair justice systems that still hadn't changed. Many other artists left the message in their music to make the individual difference like Michael Jackson. He left a hit, "Make that Change," that hit the world by storm, sending a clear message, that the world needed to change for the next generation, did it happen? and my next question, why not?

Why so much chaos and bondage on this planet, mentally, physically, and spiritually and emotionally, it makes you think, why would anyone want that kind of world? Many brilliant music artists, movie producers, magazines, newspaper industries, book artists, poetic writers all left messages, then and now. They left messages that also had a change of heart that said they wanted to help the world heal through the vibration of love and awareness.

Well, I think we all know and agree that this world here in America needs to change. Yes, this world needs a change of heart, individually and positively, for all the good of humanity. As the world change with our help, it's important to do research, on the political parties, that run this nation, it is very important to know what role the Democrat party plays politically, just as well what role, does the Republican party plays politically and it is just as important to know about independent rights.

Although this government system, seems so divided, right-wing and left-wing, whatever you want to call it, both wings are on the same "chicken," if you ask me.

These government groups are organized, by federal district branches, legislative-executive, and judicial vested, by the U.S. constitution and, congress. They play their role very well on an epic scale, of world change, with the government dictations, and legislative agendas.

Yes, it's important to know who is your Congress, and what laws they are passing, does your vote count?

Really, that is something you must ask yourself. You must know all of what Congress and legislation decide affects our reality, yes for decades to come. So if any of these laws are orchestrated in a manner of sorcery and illusion, people will always be led astray because they are clueless when it comes to seeing evil dictation, yes many are clueless, and fashionist attitude feel, we the people can be clued in later after all the mandatory laws and bills has been passed, right? and you will be told to find a way, to live with it, that's the American way, compromising, live with it or die trying, yes it seems pretty harsh but is that our reality?

Sorcery never helped the US economy grow, instead, it did the opposite, it created chaos and left a lot of shame on the land, yes, many celebrities, and church bishops faced public shaming, they all played, a role individually in this society, how they shaped it with their actions.
If Congress, and legislation and politicians and scientist, are paid off, just to make them pass laws, then there is no real legislation, just illusions everywhere, with no real

meaning to life just a masquerade ball, that we have all been invited to. Wow that means everything is considered a hoax, or we are here just being counted as sheep for the slaughter, what do you think? A paid-off Congress and legislation with a Negative mindset, could never create harmony, instead, it creates chaos globally, and who wants to keep living in that kind of world decade after decade? Now it seems it will only be by force, yes because other people choose to use the energy and time negatively on this planet, and many also force others to live a certain way, that they don't want to live like, and that's not looking out for all of humanity. That kind of thinking, can only bring in the narrative for the ones making all the rules, but we know that is mentally insane, nature didn't design for human individuals to enslave other human individuals, that's why it will only be by force? Once again, the Mind is "All." Keep it, it belongs to you.

I know many of you won't off the rollercoaster ride, we have been on for too many decades, the roller coaster ride that has no vision for peace, justice, propriety, reciprocity, harmony, order, and righteousness in your life.

As the world change, we are now faced with the 2020 year that has already rolled in, chaos, and pandemic, has the United States on a rollercoaster, and everybody is sick of riding it. Not to mention all the face masks, full of throw up, the stench of hot breath everywhere under these masks, breaking the immune system down even more every day because the nose is the filter. The good news, it's not the people's fault, this pandemic was pushed on the people in such a way, as if the USA, created the mental virus themselves, instead of China, we all know many people say it was created in the laboratory just like all the other man-made viruses and diseases. It's no secret what I'm saying, if it doesn't register in your mind, do a little research, to bring yourself up to level, on the facts, how man-made diseases are created.

On the other hand, we were told someone ate a bacterium that was contagious, a virus that attacks the lungs, although they ingested the bacteria, it could spread to other people, if you inhaled someone's breath, that was contagious with this bacterium, and somehow their contagious breath can cause mucus to build up in your lungs and turn into a virus, that someone ate by eating an animal like a bat. Ok, did this pandemic deceive billions of people? Or did all these people get sick and only get diagnosed at the hospital, people were not falling out, but they were getting diagnosed, and people were and still is Bing separated, from family, and millions have died alone with strangers, that said they were looking out for your best interest before anyone died.... Ok, all of this because someone ate a bacterium in China, that was said to be the coronavirus. That's what they are telling the world. Life will play its timeline out no doubt, and conspiracy or not, all plans, good or bad, comes to reality, and right there you will find the truth.

It seems like narcissistic groups and individuals are running the show when it comes to this pandemic, and no doubt you can feel certain people have no empathy for human life where is the soul or heart for humanity.

Just look around. We have all been invited to a global masquerade, spiritual warfare of chaos. Now the 2020/2021 elections are here, and at this time it's best you stay focused, this 2021 year has rolled in with venges it feels like. The majority of people I encounter say, "Yes," this a change like we've never seen before you can feel humanity is being threatened.

I know we all can't help but notice the change in the United States, at this point everyone faces a dilemma on an epic scale every day just to survive, that's why more so right now it's beneficial for you to stay aware of everything that is unfolding, right now as you read or listening to this audio, yes decisions are being made about the American people's, present and future right now. My question is what kind of President, and what kind of world, are we going to be dealing with? This 2020/2021 Election will bring about cause and effect like never before, and change will be present, positively, and negatively, the outcome on who becomes president here in the United States will make all the difference for these communist parties for years to come, majority of the political party, are sitting and stand by quietly, as everything unfold on to the public.

We citizens will face this reality every four years and the reality of that is, these electors that run for election every four years, make you wonder who you can trust, do these politicians really have the best interest at heart for the American people, to thrive and survive. Yes, that is the harsh reality here in the United States, will they stand and hold firm to the words that they speak during an election? Once they become elected Like how many presidents will it take to screw in a light bulb, and actually get it right, will they really act on what they say? Only time would tell again, if we failed for another president and, will this election be another, the illusion of a good president, or will we get the real deal, or will it be, this is all we have to offer at this point you can take this one we elected for you, or just be independent, so what is America left to do?

Many American people conversated with me saying, a civil war is going to break out, the Democrat Party and Republican Party also known as the red states and the blue states are going to separate, each party will go in their own direction and then you will see who had the morals and most people in America are not ready for that change, that kind of chaos will divide the redcoats and the bluecoats, that mindset will collapse America fast, and I believe that's a reality no one wants to face at this point. More drama and chaos, I don't think so, this pandemic involving the coronavirus, has shown us enough how our politicians feel, about the American people, sad to say the American economy and communities are collapsing all around, year after year, and jobs are being shipped to other countries given the American youth no promising future, is that the reality we are witnessing? More and more fast-food restaurants, marijuana dispensaries, dialysis facilities, prisons, mental health, Child Protective Services, Planned Parenthood clinics, 7-11s are becoming America's new facelift here in California, with no exaggeration just look around in your community as you drive what do your America look like?

This is the reality of the new world in many epic stages. Is the change positive or is the change negative? That's the question. What are we becoming, as a unit of people that helped build America to what it is in every way imaginable, what are you doing? individually to make sure you are not consumed in the lifestyle of work, eat and get sick, then die. I say we all have a lot to offer this expanding world globally. This 2021 election will be a phenomenal change, on an epic scale but your change depends on you mentally, physically, spiritually, and emotionally. The "Mind" is All." I encourage you to stay highly aware of your thought process. Keeping your vibration high and elevating your mind on a positive thought will lead you in the right direction on what choice and decision you will make when it comes to this election or any of them for that matter.

Many people found ways to deal with this harsh reality we are faced with, a pandemic and other elections, this is a big pill for many people to swallow, but many folks have found outlets that help them to deal with this chaotic time. Here are a few outlets many people have shared with me that have helped them during this time here in this life, this matrix, this journey, this pandemic experience, whatever you want to call it that we are being faced to deal with on this day-to-day basis. Here are the outlets I was told that helped some people.

- Spiritual guidance
- Meditation
- Mental counseling
- Motivating the youth
- Helping and motivating the elders
- Helping the communities, food, clothing
- Helping animals' rights
- Speaking up politically
- Planting a garden
- Loving themselves and other people
- Writing a book
- Creating an invention

- Writing songs
- Creating movies and film production
- Painting murals
- Keeping the environment clean in the city
- Taking better care of health and wellness

And the list could go on and on, but you get the full picture. Finding these outlets, make this world a better place to inhabit individually and collectively for millions of people and many people have shared with me how they are coping. As you begin to see and feel your vibration move on your best choices and decisions in your life, your thinking will change how you view your time spent on this planet every day of your life. We all know, a well-spent day brings about happy sleep, so says Leonardo DaVinci, little do many people know life does come with instruction on how to live, most people are not taught how to survive in this simulation.

Debbie Schapiro said, "Although life doesn't come with instructions it does come with trees, sunsets, smiles, and laughter, enjoy your day." On the other hand, many motivational books in this world will lead you to a great awakening like never before. The phenomenal change is up to you. Every day is your choice if you want to claim it, if you want to wait for someone else to make choices for you just remember there is a very big possibility someone else's choices and standards may not be the best for you, and you don't want to set yourself up for disappointment.

Iyanla Vanzant, a motivational speaker, said if you really want to live your life to the fullest and realize your greatest potential, you must be willing to run the risk of making some people mad. People may not like what you do, people may not like how you do it, but these people are not living your life" YOU ARE."

Iyanla Vanzant also said, no matter what is going on in your life today, remember, it is only preparation. People come and go; situations rise and fall; it's all preparation for better things. You must stretch, reach, grow into your goodness. Without the preparation, we receive through adversity, disappointment, confusion, or pain, we could not appreciate the goodness when it arrives. She made that quote very phenomenal, and direct to the point, the" goodness" she speaks about is the phenomenal change that is invested in everyone to do so. As we move down the timeline on this epic journey of change, I feel the energy has changed, in the mind and body, where you sit, I can feel your mind letting go, of all the negative thoughts, and negative people, and circumstances around you, your valuable judgment on life-changing choice, is very epic.

It doesn't matter about your situation at this point, and how you got there, if it is a desire to move out of your current situation, do so. The same energy that brought you to this book is the same energy you can use to find a way out, mentally first, then physically if need be. You are very clever, and intelligent, it does not matter if you are rich or poor, it does not matter about skin color, you have the abundance, to be your best version, as you grow mentally, and your age is a nonfactor, as well.

Anyone can change. Yes, you are right on time with your decision and making a positive change that will last you a lifetime guaranteed. A very well-known motivational speaker goes by the name Abraham Hicks, often portals through Esther Hicks, and says, stay in the vortex you'll be glad you did; the vortex is the happy place that you only can find on the inside of you, mentally, physically, and spiritually also emotionally. Esther and Jerry Hicks also wrote a book called the" Vortex," where the law of attraction assemblies, all cooperative relationships. Yes, Vortex is a must-read book beyond measures of overstanding the journey of life we are faced with. I recommend it because it talks about you overcoming the world, with the awareness of the Law of Attraction. It's your birthright to explore the world, and it's only found inside of your mind to do so. Esther Hicks' book sheds lots of light on that peace that is invested inside of you. Although the most divine peace; comes from the thought of knowing your truth and your experience, and loving and trusting yourself with perfect peace and harmony within you. This message is very clear and designed to get you headed, in the right direction, of knowing your life is in your hands and it is up to you to make that move into trusting yourself and truly feeling and moving free about your life. Like I have stated before many, many times, you are phenomenal and I believe in you, to help make this world a better place to live, one individual at a time, with one simple thought; I can do this, I can "change". I believe individually we can come together and co-create and unleash the powers that are invested in each one of us to have a phenomenal change of heart.

As you continue reading, think for a moment or two, what it would be like if the whole world, have a phenomenal change overnight positively. It would be magic everywhere. Although facts have proven, we did have some type of negative change overnight and it was very negative the coronavirus pandemic we were forced to face.

That vibration is a very low frequency, and a very negative vibration, that created social distance, and no real unity in American people. I only mention Corona again to bring a point, that's not the change I'm talking about. I'm speaking on a positive divine intervention, for entities globally and universally to make that decision, to invest in this divine mental, phenomenal change. The whole world needs so desperately, yes, every person would feel the cosmic shift, on an epic scale mentally, physically, spiritually, and emotionally. It would bring about a whole new horizon, on a positive thought, and harmony most definitely will be present, right alone with balance, reciprocity, order, justice, propriety, and truth, that we all can play a major role in.

I know all of humanity would look and feel phenomenal when we encounter each other. Yes, it would be pleasant to treat each other with decency and respect, love, and freedoms that we are all capable of doing.

I am positive about this vision, if harmony was present, there would be no stopping the evolving evolution. Each soul on this planet is designed to partake in and discover thyself as it is designed by nature, anyway. Your soul is the guiding light that navigates you through this rim of life. Your soul grounds you to have self-love and unconditional love for all of humanity.

This kind of love that I'm talking about is a love hormone that is found in the hypothalamus that is also known as the pineal gland or the pituitary gland. This very small gland sits in the center of the brain and plays a very big role in every human being's life. This gland releases hormones like childbearing, sexual behavior, social behavior, social bonding, well-being, and much more. This kind of love is only found in the DNA that produces oxytocin. The hormone releases fluids to the brain. It gives a sensation to the body to love self and others unconditionally, and much more. Facts have proven oxytocin produces an important chemical that sends a message to the body and behavior, also to your social intention.

This hormone plays a very leading role in society today. Can you tell who's producing this hormone in their body, versus those that do not produce this hormone?

One thing I want the millenniums to know is that is a fact. The only golden rule on this plane if that ever made a difference was love. Love keeps the axle rotating on this planet. If we ever stop loving in this world, we will most definitely destroy modern-day society and all humanity would perish. Law of attraction will, with no problem, dish out what we dish in this world, because the mindset would be too low of a frequency to love anything, otherwise, there will be no need to exist without love and we wouldn't exist either way you look at the spectrum, we all know what, the opposite of love creates. who is going to live like that? who would want to?

Only the ones who could imagine that and act on it.

As you begin to make the right choices and decisions in life and began to focus on what you want out of life, your desires will attract these kinds of people with unconditional love, peace, happiness, and the list goes on and on. Staying focused on you brings manifestation and opportunity to go forward within your journey.

Soon you will see the desires of your heart. I urge you not to waste any time. This book is in your hands but who will be the Arthur and the writer of your phenomenal story. I encourage you to live the best novel of your life to the point you gradually evolve from being unsure about your change, too a made-up mind to level up and change that extraordinary thinking, to manifesting without any negative, mind that has no boundaries in their liberation, and everyone that encounters you will be honored to have met you in this lifetime for sure.

There is no better feeling in the world to know you made a phenomenal impact on the world by changing for the better. That's why it is important to encourage the youth. I want them to know the universal message is love, and to believe in your phenomenal change and mental powers that are invested in your DNA. With the world changing so fast negatively and positively, I believe in the youth to explore and expand and experience this world like never before. It has so much to offer you, and you have so much to offer if you just open your mind positively to the thought of co-creating with the rest of the world.

The knowledge that I am sharing with the youth right now, is yours to keep forever, you are the new mastermind behind the evolution, in this mental world, You have the characteristics, this generation relies on, to keep the process of the natural way of life growing, and expanding, I believe in the youth, that is here in the United States, and all around the world, this new world, to come has already changed, the millennium's way of thinking that's why, it's important for each individual, to know they play a major part.

All life matters (you) and what you do to help humanity will impact generations to come. YES, the world is dependent on your phenomenal change.

Once again you are special, I know and truly believe in you, because you are reading this message, and this is not by coincidence this book and you, was chosen in this lifetime to prepare the stage you will perform on.

You were chosen that's why you believe in yourself, and trust yourself and love yourself. You are number one. Perseverance is all you need. Knowing the mind is all, you can do nothing without it.

Never let anyone take it from you it's your God-given right, in fact, all of humanity's right on this earth, to remain in their natural mind, keeping up with the rhythm of life. Also, keep in mind there are human beings, that will remain in a low state of mind, by choice as well.

Many people do conform and submit as you can see for yourself, all over the world. Yes, you can see the low vibration and how it operates. You can see those that have joined together to continue the fear, based mindset to control the mass majority all over the world. For me, I don't have to look very hard to see individual people, accepting their phenomenal change mentally, physically, spiritually and the list goes on.

People are reinventing themselves, and expanding their possibility to go forward mentally, healthy, and happily. It all starts with you. The younger you are with a positive mindset, the better off you'll be in the future, because the here and now are here, right before our eyes whether you like it or not. This millennial generation, I'm speaking directly to you, you all count as well. It is your decision to show your phenomenal light, your energy, and your talent.

Showing the world your intelligence, and your positive action counts right now.

The power to change is invested in your DNA, forever, it can be activated with one positive thought, to change for the better, when you choose yourself, you are banking on yourself, and yes that will take you further in your journey by thinking positive, don't wait on it just do it!

CHAPTER 8

Believe in You! You Matter!

As I leave this message to the youth, please know that it is very necessary. Their liberation is being threatened as we speak. The agenda to destroy the natural things in life and bring destruction to their freedom is very epic. Once upon a time, there used to be rumors about agendas to destroy humanity and freedom of speech, and freedom to think. Yes, over the years and decades, it has proven what all conspiracy theories have been saying for decades. In fact, the agendas were not made up, as it was portrayed to, we the people.

As the conspiracy theorist proved they were not lying same 30 years later about our freedom of speech being dismantled. In fact, it was true, hid only for a certain amount of time before the truth really surfaced, I know that bugs certain groups, that know when they want their agenda to be revealed.

What I'm speaking on is nothing new, facts have proved the youth liberation is being threatened, schools are closed in the United States as we speak, evidence to show itself, this is how they start at the new world by tearing it down first, they got total online strangers teaching a class in our children's bedroom. What kind of education are they given to the future? I don't know which direction this legislation is leading the US into, but a better decision is desperately needed ASAP. What I am saying is actual and factual. The agenda is already in motion and they are looking to conquer the world with this corrupt state of mind.

Now I have come to this question, do you feel you matter in this world, or do you think you can make a difference?

Let's go deeper into facts on how you matter if you didn't know. You matter on all levels. When you hear the word "matter" it can be used in many ways, it has different definitions and meanings. Let me explain how you matter, and yes, many negative people would say your life doesn't matter, but it does my friend. So, let's see how you matter. The definition for MATTER, "Physical Substance in general, as distinct from mind and in (physics) that which occupies space and possesses rest mass, especially as distinct from energy. It's vital that you understand and then overstand why you matter. Now that you know the definition of matter, know that I'm talking about you and your greatness if that makes any sense to you.

I need you to know, and get a clear view on this matter, on this planet you take up space that belongs to your existence, your Atoms and compounds are made very small, but all our actions build the existence of everything around today. Your DNA, and your RNA, is one of the main conductors that matter to your existence. Never forget that. Your human body mass is made of six elements; oxygen, carbon, hydrogen, nitrogen, calcium, and phosphorus, only 0.85% of your body is composed of other elements; potassium, sulfur, sodium, chlorine, and magnesium, wow, that's just a few of the elements that make you phenomenon inside and out.

All those elements make you a powerhouse of matter, beautifully and wonderfully made, and no person can take that unique quality away from you, no matter how high any person, woman, or man, have placed their self above you, rich or poor, white, or black, they are still made no better than you and that's facts. With all these degrees of elements of what you are made of, no person has the right to hold you back from your greatest potential on this planet. Although there are other people who feel right now, they are better than you, they are very crafty people with a very corrupt conscience when it comes to other life. In fact, there are all kinds of egotistical traps and obstacles to block your potential in this phenomenal life we experience. In this assimilation, what a shame how some people disregard human life like garbage, like life is something to throw away, a very small group, decided to live their life on this planet to disregard other life like they don't matter. The enlightenment that I'm speaking over your life and circumstance right now is a clear message that you matter. We will never get another you. We can search the whole world and there is only one you, and that's very phenomenal my friend.

Your physical life matters and plays a role in the universe. Each electron, proton, and neutron that makes up your carbon copy, make your atoms what they are, that's why there is none like you, you only come once in a lifetime in this body. Although your energy will never die, it will transform to a higher matter of pure substance in space and energy, where time doesn't exist, only phenomenal change consistently nonstop.

Also, in this assimilation facts are proven there are 118 chemical elements, and they can change to all kinds of forms and make all kinds of matter with the mind, that's why it's so important to know, as well the mind is all mentally, physically, and spiritually.

Matter is all around just look at all the material that was made from it. I pay homage to the phenomenal people who made matter form into something they thought of, different creations and inventions, in this lifetime on this planet. Most definitely phenomenal people served their purpose in this moderate time we live in.

Whether they got the credit for their invention or not, they put their positive contribution into the world. Phenomenal individuals always leaving evidence behind that they counted like you and I also count. So yes, matter changes from one state of mind to the other state of mind mentally and physically on many degrees. As a matter of fact, your energy as well. Facts have been proven; the richest man in the world knows that you matter. Elon Musk proves how the mind is a powerful tool, it can be used in two ways good or evil, and it doesn't matter how much money you have, we all matter, and what we really spend our time doing on this plane matters that's facts.

The scientist of the world knows that your energy cannot be destroyed, no matter how hard the scientist globally tries, they can talk about global warming all day and climate control all they want, it will never work. Our ancestors have already proven you have to adapt to climate change, the energy you housed on the inside of you can only do that, that's why it's important to know we don't die we transform, or change from, one form to another, we don't die we transform, to higher energy beyond, this physical, and mental conscience world we dream in. In other words, you cannot be created or destroyed, what I am telling you, no scientist on the face of this planet can create the exact you, and they cannot destroy you, energy cannot be destroyed, it only can transform, only the flesh dies, and Infinity and beyond brings a new horizon to your physical experience that you have on this planet.

The universe is made up of atoms that float in space, dark matter, dark energy, normal matter, that consist of Atoms that make up, stars, planets, human beings, and every other visible object in the Universe if you were to move up in the sky, like on an airplane, or even a so-called, space ship, listen to that word, (space) (ship) you will see everything around you change into atoms and even disappear to the all-seeing eye and that's facts. So yes, know that space and the present you hold is very epic, on all scales of life, open your mind and set yourself free to inner standing, that you are limitless and, nothing and no one has the right to hold you down or up, to something you are forced to do and didn't agree to. Your energy is the best-sustained truth to your physical or mental activity. Always be aware of the energy that is invested in you. Many people know on this plane your energy matters to them, also your DNA and RNA, why because there are two main types of energy; negative and positive energy, also known as potential and kinetic energy, which one is you?

Well, most people know your potential energy is stored in your body, and your kinetic energy is in use with what you do, so don't waste your energy on anyone, or any projects you're not dedicated to. Once again, which energy field are you working with? Ask yourself how you use your energy. Positive or negative in this world we dream in. The reality is they cannot create the natural energy or destroy your natural energy, only the flesh can be put down to dust, but never the energy within you, you will face phenomenal change. Everyone's energy will transform from flash two, kinetic energy, it's always and constantly moving. Once again you will never die. How phenomenal is that, yes you will experience this body in this divine universal oneness.

That's why I have no problem saying Infinity and beyond because it is actual and factual. That's what makes us infinite, my readers, unlimited in time and space, boundless as well as the stars, too many to count. Your energy Is too large to contain on this planet, you cannot be bound, even if you are in a place where it looks as if, you are never going to get out of that place and space, you will, nothing is forever, that's facts.

For example, if you are on a job, or incarcerated, or in a toxic relationship, or some type of unpleasant space, you're not bound, although there are certain people who want you to believe and feel hopeless, and even if you feel that way and it seems that way, you still are not bound my friend, "the mind is all."

Just remember you are infinite, and if you don't know what that means, look it up for your well-being. I say this with all diligence, never put yourself in an unhealthy position that will allow anyone to manipulate your energy, in this lifetime, it is all yours, and no matter where you are in this world, it's your divine living right to express yourself, your energy, your light, your matter, so let your energy shine to the highest version of you, I believe in you. I will never doubt anyone in this life that shares this infinite time and space with myself and the rest of the world, although we all have many paths to go down, it will all lead us back to the universal oneness, that connects us all on this plane. Never forget the mind is all, also it's a very powerful tool, to the elite who control the media perception on an epic level, and they know this my beloved friend.

I know I have talked about phenomenal change so much, you may feel it already, and ready to make that change, that will last a lifetime for yourself, and for the better of all humanity, in the most epic way possible, it is in your power and capability, you know so, and do so, I believe in you and everyone around you to reach their full potential at being the best version of yourself. So, bring your talent, your skills, to the table of love, peace, balance, harmony, propriety, reciprocity, justice, order, yes bring, all those attributes, and you will see a whole new world, that will change for the better, for all living things on this plane. I could go on about all kinds of change that need to happen, but we all get the universal message.

CHAPTER 9

Healthier for Your Change

This last but not the least of messages, it's about the food we consume on a day-to-day basis. This change is a very epic change, and very important to your phenomenal change. what we eat, and consume in our body, is the number one important, key conductor to a healthy functioning body.

All life on this planet needs a healthy maintained food diet. The nourishment that we need, to maintain a healthy body is "nutrients." Let's go deeper into knowing what the word nutrient means. The definition for the word nutrient is a plural noun; a substance that provides nourishment essential for growth and maintenance of life. Now the substance it's talking about, is protein, vitamins, and minerals. Why is that so important? And the most important nutrients the pro hormone is vitamin D. Vitamin D, fights against all bacteria and viruses and disease your immune system is best healthy when you are vitamin D sufficiency. Always remember keeping a healthy body prevents sickness, the body is a living organism, and you helping your body nourishment is very much needed, in the tissues of the body. Six nutritious foods your body really need are,

Carbohydrates Liquids

(FAT) Proteins Vitamin D Minerals Water

These, nutrients, helps build strong, bones, and teeth. The minerals turn the food you eat, into energy, so the body can work properly. Also don't forget to include calcium, iron, and potassium, that helps fight off any disease or disorder in the body. The most important out of these three is (IRON), it carries the oxygen throughout the body to the red blood cells) and provides hemoglobin and myoglobin, a protein the muscle needs. Iron is essential for activating certain enzymes, that produces amino acids, collagen, neurotransmitters, and yes, our hormones need, the oxygen magnesium produces, and provides for the body, that's what gives us calcium that, builds bone, and teeth and much more. Perhaps someone may say at this moment what does that have to do with phenomenal change!

You are one with your body, we all know the mind can do nothing without a physical body, so what we put in our body, as far as food, medications and vaccines are concerned, can change the hole DNA, and RNA, condition negatively and positively, and an unhealthy body, could lead to unhealthy thoughts, and that's facts.

Look around the world in this simulation we eat in, you can name some, of the places off the top of your head, we see them everywhere, and what are the main choices of foods you see? Are they healthy, are those fast-food restaurants causing more harm than good? The new facelift of surrounding cities in America is actually made up of dialysis, restaurants, fast food, pharmacies, marijuana dispensary's everywhere if you live here in California, but getting back to the subject, we all are witnessing sickness skyrocketing, on many levels, mentally, and physically, we all know that making the wrong food choice, can cause many illness, and sometimes generational illness can be passed down to your children, through the RNA, that is designed to change and manipulate the DNA that's facts. With all the fast- food take out, put before your eyes, to consume, I don't recommend an unhealthy diet, for our nutrient, it can leave you with an acidic body that will deteriorate you inside out. It's very epic you know the symptoms, that can lead you too, an unhealthy body and make your body immune system react, to inflammatory illnesses, feelings symptoms like:

- Bloating
- Bloody or black stool
- Blood in vomit

- Constantly burping
- Dysphagia
- Sensations like food stuck in the throat
- Nausea after eating
- Weight gain or loss
- Wheezing
- Dry cough after eating
- Chronic sore throat and virus

This list could go on and on, but you get the clear picture, right?

You are what you eat! And those are just a few symptoms that let you know; you are dealing with an acidic body.

If you are dealing with any of those symptoms, it's best to start on a healthy diet now, there is nothing wrong with continuing to strive, for the best alkaline body, you want to see. Many people feel they can eat, whatever they want, that's true as well, but what choice do you think, is the healthy one for you. So recently the News, reported, many people are eating unhealthily when it comes to food choices. Right now, all over the world, we are being told, a virus came all the way from, China, to the US, and it has spread to other countries as well, threatening humanity as we speak, because of a bacterium found in animals such as, cats, dogs, rats, bats, horses, monkeys, Tigers, and bears, oh my, etc.

When you consume this kind of animal meat you make your body a powerhouse for disease, bacteria, virus, parasites, and fungi, that transmit to humans from animals, internally. Also, when bestiality, practices are involved with having sex with any animal, you can transmit any disease or bacteria, these viruses can carry many parasites, to the human tissue, that can cause you to be a host for a major virus, like the one coronavirus, aka Covid-19. A certain, small group of individuals are telling the world a virus came out of China in a town called Wuhan. This virus they say, broke out in a market that, sold animals goods, that people choice to consume on a daily. As I have stated before, this kind of eating, is not a good or great, source of nourishment, fore your body, there is a danger that, a bacterial, infection, like anthrax, hepatitis, also leptospirosis it can spread through the meat to the person, that is consuming this animal. So, I wouldn't recommend this idea for nourishment, or pleasurable eating, for that matter at all. This Corona outbreak in the US, has petrified millions of people, millions have fell victim to this so-called Corona outbreak, and it was transmitted through animal consuming, it let the hole, world know, it was not a healthy choice for whoever was eating, this way in China, in fact anywhere around the world just for, pleasurable eating, these practices, customs, and unusual ways and behaviors and sinister rituals involving animal blood and eating human meat it's definitely not nourishment.

Cannibalism and drinking blood of any sort, even to pretend drinking blood or eating flash, isn't a good act either, that's not a healthy mind set mentally either, pretending to drink blood on any Sunday program is to be thought out and research to find out where that ritual history comes from, think about it, what are you doing to yourself, mentally physically and spiritually, what kind of ritual programming and religious systems have you gotten into, that requires you to eat or drink sacrificed blood. This is something to think about because clearly, this way of eating, does the opposite to your body it, bring sickness and disease, and these blood rituals, are no longer necessary, in this modern time we dream in.

This way of eating has been proven, that this is, a way of mentally thinking, not a way of living and it has been made the normal. I had to share with you, how you eat can make all the difference in your everyday life, it should never be taking for granted, mentally or physically. This message from the universe, sends a clear message, about this so-called Corona virus, it's not always in your best interest to consume pleasurable meat for a source of nourishment, it can lead to much more disinterring consequences, as you can see, in today's media, no matter if it's true or a hoax it is being said to influence the mass majority.

Facts proven, 72 billion, animals are slaughtered each year on land, and 1.2 trillion aquatic animals, are killed for food, all around the world every year, for pleasurable eating, for the food chain, yes mankind eat this way every year, and how could we possibly think, that is ok with the universe, and the Divine God of love.

Many people were exposed, for this lifestyle and for this way of thinking and eating on an epic scale. This so called, Coronavirus is being blamed for all the fear, chaos, social distance, and mask wearing we are faced with right now. I know much of what I'm saying is hard to believe but it is proven, it is facts, research is always at your fingertips. In the United States, there is a health crisis, because the choices individuals are choosing when it comes to food and knowledge of food. Remember, I told you "The mind is all," you can do nothing without it. Your phenomenal change depends on you, and your health is one of the key factors, to your mental, physical, and spiritual health, it's up to you to nourish your body in the most, healthiest, way possible that will last you a lifetime, of good health and healthy choices.

What I love about nature, it has provided, the right nourishment, all our human existence on this planet, there is an abundance of natural food, that is provided on this planet, every year. Nature provides a normal, and practical way of satisfying your appetite, by simply turning to nature for those substance and nourishment the way nature intended it.

This message once again is very clear and direct, if we don't recognize our position in humanity, we will all face destruction in the worst way in this simulation, we call life. There will be no future, it won't be there, without a healthy mind set, to carry on the human legacy, that everything in nature matters, and counts and that's facts.

This Universal message is very real, and everything I have written about, yes, this message is from, the "ONE TRUE GOD," The, "Christ" has divinely moved in energy, and spoken in spirit, to me on this matter, yes, for me to right this book, this universal message, for all of us, to have this, divine, phenomenal change, inside and out, for the better for humanity and self, so we all can, continue inhabiting this simulation we thrive in. We all occupied this space and place of existence all over this world.

Geo- graphics have proven it is more than enough space to go around for billions of crops to be produced, yet small groups of people, wont it all for them self's, doing anything they find necessary to stay on top, of the world's perception, to keep this illusion going, globally. It's disappointing to say but that's what a very low vibration, mind set thinks like, all day a bound mind, can't think but one way and it's not positive.

From another point of view, we all clearly can see, nature looks as if it's losing the battle to keep humanity existing, because of these small groups of people, on this planet but , truth is this world will continue to expand and grow, and discoveries, that are yet to be discovered, will emerge, this is why it's important to keep the vibration of love in your thoughts with everything you do, for self and love for other's to continue to show it's truth in us all in this simulation, matrix, world, universe, life, journey, experience, whatever you want to call it, it will grow that's why, this space, and place is pleading with you, is pleading with us all of us. These time's we are living in, cannot be taking lightly, rich, or poor it doesn't matter if it's the governments, or legislation, it doesn't matter what background you come from or what kind of high position, you were placed in, this world bondage, has to stop.

I believe and know, that all humans on this planet, are all capable, and have the ability to do so, and yes, it is necessary.

I'm here to help open your mind to your phenomenal change. And I truly know you can do it!

CHAPTER 10

God's of Love

My last encouraging message: life was designed this way by the true source, that created this world we learned to love in. I heard the knock, and I answered the door. For all the individuals, or groups, that heard the knock and truly open their hearts, with pure, true intent to love the world, congratulations you made it through, this universal message, you heard it and answered the door. Yes, your phenomenal change and experience will be the best phenomenal change of your existence. You are now on your way to a better version of yourself, in a different form of respect, for yourself and the world, and respect for natural love, yes you are, the true (I AM) it's (YOU).

The powers and the knowledge and good forces are invested in your DNA. You are GODS of true love, that comes from the GODS OF LOVE on this planet seen and unseen. Yes, you can clearly tell the GODS of Evil, the way its practice, they are deceitful and full of hidden agenda, destroying and taking over the natural resources that God provided in nature. Nature represents the true love of GOD and GODS people. Love and evil aren't the same, and a GOD of love, would not stand back and watch evil take place, so the I AM, have to move by the spirit, and flow with the great energy that, sends a positive impact, in this world. Yes, you are the instruments and fabric that keep and make this earth vibrates to a humble and peaceful tune, and yes you can clearly see the magnitude of each action that goes forward negatively and positively on this planet.

Counterfeit love is always present, that's their job, the pretender, it has nothing to do with heaven or hell, it's all a state of mind, and yet a pretender, the heart is full of deception, these individuals speak volumes, with their actions globally keeping the raft of deception going, playing a very wicked game with a delusional ill will and intent, playing the mass majority, with no true intentions to love the world at all. These pretenders, intentions to profit in the most negative way, playing with the mass majority minds and DNA, turning it into RNA to manipulating the natural genetic code made by nature.

There is no sugar coating the truth. You can taste it for yourself, and trust me when I say, the taste is a bitter and unpleasant lifestyle, and a mindset of corruption to be in, no thanks. I choose pure love; I choose to vibrate on the highest vibration that exists on this plane, riding this cosmic wave into eternity into the black hole. Mastering your awakening is up to you, also this world depends on your self-love. My final words are coming to an end. In this book, this message, has been a phenomenal change in my life. And I am grateful in this lifetime, to be a spiritual being having a human experience, also a multi, dimensional human being having a human experience, we are all just passing through, in this lifetime, make your experience count, what kind of legacy will you leave to the new generations to come?

MY MISSION STATEMENT

I am honored in this lifetime to exist in an epic way. I was able to see the light that shined so bright for me. I was born with the crown of glory around my head when I push through my mother's portal, also known as my mother's womb. Yes, being born into this matrix, that was the beginning of my journey's walk in this life.

The lens I see through has seen the world in a divine way, from above, not from the eyes down below, but from the conscience universe and universes from above and below us. I dwale mentally, where all creations exist phenomenally, were the "DIVINE ONE", dwells, were the conscience knows we all count. My mission is to be the best version of myself, every day of my existence, never taking it for granted, that I am a part of this phenomenon, that is taking place, in the universal conjunction, heavens, world, universe, cosmos, mind, body, it's simply designed this way. I live, thrive, experience, life in the flash, mentally, physically, and spiritually. Let me not forget emotionally. I am honored to have experienced all these elements and degrees that life has to offer. This universal consciousness that I have learned to trust and partake in has given me quite a journey and lessons to learn from. In this world it's my moral duty, my obligation, my responsibility, to the generations after me yes, it's very epic, and to the generations before me it is very vital to leave this message to the world.

Right now, governors and legislation are threatening humanity globally. As you read or listen to this audio, there is an agenda in full motion to depopulate and destroy the natural laws in the universe. Facts has been proven onto me in this lifetime, media, newspapers, magazines, music, family, friends, hospitals, presidents, governors, legislation, can be the worst enemy to a thriving and expanding, growing world that has trusted these parties and entities for decades. I learned If they conscience vibrate negatively and corrupt driven, then you can't follow that kind of mindset in this lifetime "NO WAY". When you can't trust the various entities and institutions that told us we can trust them, and they have our best interest at heart for the people, but in the actions of these parties they have shown there is a discrepancy in the way they are orchestrating them self in this world, it doesn't help the conscience growth, globally or universal.

This is the main reason why I must continue to pave the way, and do the opposite of destruction, and to be my best version, to be a part of this existing world, others have this same obligation as well. Yes, all over the world that is our obligation to society. Facts have been proven life has a long history on this planet, and our ancestors also new. yes, we also existed before this modern time we dwale in today, our ancestors, left hieroglyphics, stones and carving, paving the way for our modern day, we dwell in, leaving evidence that this planet and the life on it has seen many revolutions come and go, yes, they existed and left hundreds, of civilizations, all over the globe, for us to discover, leaving all kinds of powerful symbols behind that are used to this day, yes there was lots of evidence.

So yes, it's an honor in this lifetime and I got the opportunity to co- create with 9 billion people and more perhaps, but my point is we all inhabit and share this planet. yes, the process of life, the way it expresses itself, shows how phenomenal each person is. I found that it is necessary and very vital how I chose to use my time and my energy at this present. I chose to keep it simple, to see this life clearly, my full 360 degree the reason for living to experience this conscience energy, that we dwell in, in this lifetime. My metamorphosis is the renewing of my mind 360-degree full circle, will count in this simulation.

I choose not to spend my life in vain, but the opposite, to be very fruitful to myself and all of humanity.

My phenomenal change has been worth it all, and I can see the value to myself and others.

I pay homage to, the one mind of love, that moves, with grace on this planet, I pay homage to the good forces that never gives up on the spirit of love, the vibration of love that continues to carry on this spiritual phenomenon, and mental battle, for individuals' mindsets to be completely liberated, on all levels of mental bondage, spiritual bondage, physical bondage, and emotional bondage, yes, I pay homage to those forces.

I am so honored, in this lifetime, I didn't choose to take the road, of being a maniac or a psychopath, having no empathy and remorse for natural genetic coding we call life.

Yes, we are all having the same experience, or are we having the same experience? When it comes to flesh and blood? Although I know the egotistical, maniac, and psychopath, can also have a phenomenal change, of heart as well, as it was designed, giving you the choice to change the heart from an evil mind set to a loving heart, this is the main reason why we are conscience to evil, in this dimension, we have a choice, although evil is taught and exist, remember, it is a lot of energy that goes into teaching people that way of thinking, anyone can follow by example to be evil minded, or should I say brainwashed to create destruction for other human life or is it passed through the bloodline? Yes, you have the power to make a choice, to love or be evil it's that simple. What path will you take? My mission is to experience love and all the degrees that it expresses itself, as I love my self and others. "THANK YOU"

We are infinite power expressing, infinite love, infinite energy, we are limitless, there is no measure or limit to your, "PHENOMENAL CHANGE", YES YOU MADE IT. I KNEW LOVE COULD COUNT ON YOU, I KNEW THE WORLD COULD COUNT ON YOU AS WELL. THANKS FOR BELIEVING IN

YOURSELF, not just believing but knowing who you are and what you want out of life. I am honored to know "THE NATURAL THINGS" matter on an epic scale, YES, MY FRIENDS, YOUR LIFE HAS SO MUCH TO OFFER THE WORLD, LIKE LIBERTY AND THE RIGHT TO PURSUE HAPPINESS... It was an honor to be chosen to write this message in this lifetime, leaving my own phenomenal blueprint of my Rosetta stone. I GIVE THANKS TO INFINITE EXISTENCE AND EXPERIENCE THAT WE DREAM IN...

POEM BY: Jonathan Lamar Boyd

It was selfish of me to think the World can change overnight. I understand that now.

So, I will accept the fact that this, is. A process and no matter how much I would like for it to speed up. It won't

The world does not revolve. Around me
Just wishing and thinking Day after day
Night after night When will we change?

Can we actually learn to live? Without violence, hatred etc...?
I've tried suppressing these. Thoughts yet my heart continues. To ask what matter?
My mind keeps moving in and out. Of the illusion
My thoughts are ruined.
The more I see.
The more I understand.
Along with understanding comes clarity. Clarity results to purpose

The appreciations of purpose bring on responsibility.
Responsibility requires tolerance.
In order to remain tolerant, one has to become humble.
One becomes humble due wisdom.
Wisdom arises from maturity.

Maturity growth is a product of experience. So, if we change our reality.
Our experience of life

We can forever change the world how. We perceive reality.
Life is what you make of it. So collectively with our minds
We create this world.
We choose to suffer.

We choose to live violently. We choose our illusion. We are the creators of our world. We are the GOD'S. We are our demons.

Ultimately that would mean we are our heroes!

This poem speaks volumes, when it comes to the decisions that we make when we are creating our reality, in fact we are our own hero's, at the end of the day, you cannot rely on anyone to come and save you, the process begins in your mind, and you must save yourself mentally before you can save anyone else, remember you are your own demon and hero at the same time, which of the two energy you rather let take over your mind and action?

Life changing, Quotes to live by:

"We do not need magic to change the world, we carry all the power we need inside ourselves already: we have the power to imagine better."

Let us remember: One book, one pen, one child, and one teacher can change the world." (Malala Yousufzai)

Never doubt that a small group of thoughtful, committed citizens can change the world; indeed, it's the only thing that ever has… (Margaret Mead)

Together we can change the world, just one random act of kindness at a time. (Ron Hall

Every moment is an organized opportunity, every person a potential activist, every minute a chance to change the world. (Dolores Huerta)

You can't change the world alone- you will need some help- and to truly get from your starting point to your destination it takes friends, colleagues, the good will of strangers and a strong coxswain to guide them. (William H. McRaven)

We are all one. People are interconnected by an invisible force. Although we have the freedom to think and act, we stick together, like the stars in the heavenly arc, with unbreakable connections. These connections cannot be seen, but we can feel them." (Nikola Tesla)

Let the future tell the truth, let it judge each man according to his work and merit. The present is theirs, but the future is mine, the future for which I worked so hard." (Nikola Tesla)

Young people have the imagination to change the world, some of you adults can learn a lot from a child, by using your imagination to do so … (Gloria B. Daniels)

No one never mentions how change feels often, but we all know how pain feels, so what kind of change will you deal into this changing world. (Gloria B. Daniels)

If You change the way you look at things, the things you look at change. (Wayne Dyer) "The state of your life is nothing more than a reflection of your state of mind". (Wayne Dyer)

"We should never have to pay a negative price to change, because change will never charge you a dime to think positive in this world, it's your choice it's your free will to do so". (Gloria B. Daniels)

www.ingramcontent.com/pod-product-compliance
Lightning Source LLC
Chambersburg PA
CBHW031251290426
44109CB00012B/528